MW00613538

Self-Publishing for the First-Time Author

An Author Your Ambition Book

by M.K. Williams

ISBN: 978-1-7333929-3-8 (Paperback)
Library of Congress Control Number: 2020900835

All content reflects our opinion at a given time and can change as time progresses. All information should be taken as an opinion and should not be misconstrued for professional or legal advice. The contents of this book are informational in nature and are not legal or tax advice, and the authors and publishers are not engaged in the provision of legal, tax, or any other advice.

Printed by MK Williams Publishing, LLC in the United States of America.

First printing edition 2020.

authoryourambition@gmail.com

www.authoryourambition.com

Works by M.K. Williams

Fiction

The Project Collusion Series
Nailbiters
Architects

The Feminina Series
The Infinite-Infinite
The Alpha-Nina

Other Fiction
The Games You Cannot Win
Escaping Avila Chase
Enemies of Peace

Non-Fiction

Self-Publishing for the First-Time Author
Book Marketing for the First-Time Author
How to Write Your First Novel: A Guide for Aspiring Fiction Authors
Going Wide: Self-Publishing Your Books Outside The Amazon Ecosystem
The Fiology Workbook

Table of Contents

Dedication:
To all the aspiring authors who dream, plan, write, and work hard to make it a reality.

Self-Publishing for the First-Time Author

An Author Your Ambition Book

Introduction

My Story

In late 2013, I attended a local author's workshop at a library near my home. I had written two novels by this time, and I had failed to secure any interest from a literary agent. Getting an agent is the first step in the traditional publishing process, after writing your novel. I was excited to be able to speak with a local author who had gone through the entire publishing process to hear what I should look out for; any tips on what I could do to improve my query letters. I was ready to learn the ins-and-outs of publishing. I did see that the author's work was not in my genre, so I knew asking for her agent's contact information wouldn't make sense. I understood going in that any advice she gave would be specific to her genre. But I figured at a minimum that we could chat and I could learn something from her.

I didn't know any other local authors at the time. I was looking for connection and community. I was looking for answers.

What happened was the exact opposite.

I sat through her presentation and patiently waited for the Q&A portion. I asked what advice she had for anyone starting out on the publishing journey. She looked at me and said, "You're what? 23? What could you possibly have to say?"

I was stunned. I could not believe that this woman who didn't even know me had dismissed me so casually. She not only didn't want to help me, she thought I had nothing to say just because of my age, because of how I looked.

I was crushed. I didn't write for a few months. How could I reach my goal of having my book published, when I didn't know how to get there? There was no information out there to help me figure it out. Or at least, I hadn't found it yet.

It was my husband who noticed that I had been disconnected and uninspired. He saw that I hadn't been spending my weekends writing as much and asked me why. He inquired if getting a publishing deal was the goal, or if having a published book was the goal? I looked at him like he had twelve heads. "Those are the same thing!" He smiled and then asked if I had even considered self-publishing. I balked. He did not understand. I couldn't do that. If I self-published then I would never get a publishing deal. "Research it, do the work to prove that it isn't a valid option for you. Then go back and work on the traditional route."

My husband and I are both very ambitious, Type-A people. When he issued a challenge like that I had to respond and prove to him that I was right (but in a very loving, 'I told you so' manner). I set out to do my research. And the information I found wasn't what I had expected. When I was in college I had briefly looked into self-publishing. I had taken one look at a website that offered offset print runs of 1,000 books, saw the sticker price, and closed out of the browser.

But the second time around I saw that there were services that offered print-on-demand books; I would not have the upfront costs or the inventory. There was access to publish directly with major retailers. My husband was right: self-publishing was a viable option. Popular books like *50 Shades of Grey* and *The Martian* had started as self-published efforts that gained traction after growing an online audience. I swallowed my pride, told him that he was right, and set about the task of writing my third novel. That novel was *Nailbiters*, and it became my first self-published book.

When I set out to publish that book in 2015, I spent

hours scouring the internet for information. My limited research in 2013 had given me the confidence to self-publish, but now I needed the nitty-gritty details. How could I get my book out to major retailers and make sure libraries across the nation would accept it? How much was all of this going to cost? What pitfalls were waiting for me? I have condensed my years of experience into this book so that you don't have to spend your precious time looking everywhere for one answer.

I took time away from writing and editing to learn each of these details. Self-publishing is not for the faint of heart. You are effectively becoming a one-person writing, publishing, publicity, distribution, and sales enterprise. While this sounds daunting, many don't realize that traditional publishers still require their authors to do much of their own marketing and publicity. When you self-publish you add on some work, but you retain all your rights and royalties.

When I first investigated this avenue, it was clear that there was still a stigma around self-publishing. Every agent I had queried when I looked into traditional publishing had clear warnings on their websites: do not apply if you have self-published previously. I thought that this would be a mar on my publishing permanent record. I later realized that being self-published would make me a bad client because then I would know the questions to ask, the payment structure to negotiate, and all the small details that they would probably prefer I didn't check into. The idea that self-published authors are "taking the lazy way out" has long since been refuted. Most people now appreciate the level of effort and business acumen needed to succeed at self-publishing. As traditionally published authors look to self-publish their next book, the publishing industry is poised to change once more.

The reason that I am telling you this is to let you know that there has never been a better time for you to self-publish your book. The availability of information, print and distribution options, and community support has never been better. It has certainly improved over the years as I have published my own books.

Your Story

To get you started, I am going to break down the information that will be the most helpful to you in the process. How will readers consume your book? Where will they be able to purchase it or rent it? How can you make sure it is set up correctly? What costs are associated with this process? What are the best strategies for launching your book to ensure sales and reviews?

These are all questions I had many years ago. I will give you answers based on my experience and expertise. Your strategy will be unique to you, the book you write, and the audience you serve. Your plan for self-publishing is specific to your book, your genre, and your vision for your career as an author.

Through this book, I am going to walk you through the steps that you will need to take to self-publish your book. We will start with some plans that you may have already started to form during the writing stage and then move right into editing, formatting, and hitting publish.

You can come back to this book at each step in the process to review any details that you may need a refresher on. You can also visit **AuthorYourAmbition.com/Videos** to see my tutorials for specific platforms to help you navigate the important websites.

Your journey as a self-published author starts now. Whether you just decided to take the leap and make your book a reality, or if you have several traditionally published books on the market and you are looking to gain control of your creative work: this book is designed to help you jump over the initial hurdles and get your book self-published!

So, let's get started, people want to read your book, they just don't know it yet.

Chapter 1:

My Book is Complete! Now What?

It can seem like a daunting journey to go from first draft to printed and published book. After you complete that first draft you should take a moment and celebrate. There is always more work to do with your book, and while it may be "done," you will never finish working to promote it. Celebrate along the way and enjoy each step of the process.

Now that you have taken in the excitement of this moment, you'll take the first step towards self-publishing. It is time to determine what formats your book will be available in.

Pick Your Format(s) First

You have likely had several daydreams of what it would be like to see someone reading your book. Do you picture walking into a local bookstore and picking your book off the shelf? Do you envision looking over at the screen of your neighbor on a subway or plane and seeing them scrolling through your book on their eReader app?

Chances are you already know what formats you *want* to publish your book in. But what are the best formats for your book based on your audience and publishing plan? I have worked with clients who had a very specific vision of walking to their neighborhood Barnes & Noble and seeing their book on the shelves. That dream was clear and so our publishing plan was built around making that possible. When their book signing at their local Barnes & Noble sold out, I knew we had made their dream a reality.

Other clients wanted to create a workbook that someone could actually write in. That led to a very different discussion on formatting than if they had wanted their book strictly for leisure reading.

The reason we are looking at the formatting first is that decisions you make in editing will be impacted by the formats you select for publishing. Are there links that will be clickable in an eBook, but that clearly won't do anything in a print version? Are there graphs and images that will need to be described for an audio format?

Keep in mind that with any of the formats you select to self-publish with, you can add more later. If you want to dip your toes in the self-publishing waters you can start with one format, then add another once you feel more comfortable. Yes, it may be ideal to launch with all formats on day one, but that is very hard to coordinate. If you are working a full-time job while trying to publish your first book: give yourself some grace and stick with one thing at a time.

Below is a review of each major format:

eBook

That's right, I'm starting with eBooks and not print books. Because self-publishing became accessible to the masses when eBooks arrived. In terms of a printing revolution, I would posit that the dawn of eBooks is second only to Johannes Gutenberg's invention of the printing press. Before personal electronic devices were readily available to the masses, the only way to read books was via a hardcover or paperback. Audiobooks existed as massive CD collections. Books were clunky, heavy, and took a lot of time and resources to produce.

Then eBooks arrived. When Barnes & Noble released

Nook and Amazon released its first Kindle, the publishing world changed. People demanded an easy way to read books. You can now carry an entire library in your pocket. And, in terms of self-publishing, authors could now release their books in a digital format. Readers wanted eBooks and self-publishers stepped in to answer the demand.

Most self-published authors start out with their work available in eBook format and add on other formats as they see fit. That matches my own story. When I was looking to self-publish, I did the research and saw how many options I had for getting an eBook out to the world. The print options were a bit more limited and the idea of managing inventory seemed daunting and expensive. But eBooks were becoming more popular. I could publish my book as an eBook and start to make some revenue from my hard work. The eBook would be my proof of concept.

As an author, you will most likely have an eBook version of your book. The exceptions would be if you publish a coloring book or a journal that has an interactive component where a person has to put pen to paper to get the value.

A few notes about my personal experience with eBooks:

People don't like trees...

A big factor for only releasing my first two books as eBooks was my stubborn belief that all book readers were like me. I am a very frugal person; I don't want to spend more than I have to. I assumed that if readers had an option between an eBook at $0.99 or a paperback at any cost above that, they would want the eBook. I also thought I was a warrior for the environment and protecting trees by only publishing a digital version of my book.

When my third book came out, I was finally comfortable enough with the print-on-demand (POD) options to release it in both paperback and eBook. This meant that copies of my books would only be printed and paper used if and when a book was ordered. Guess what happened? The paperback far outsold the eBook. Subsequently, I released a paperback version for the first two books at a higher price point and guess what? Those sold better than the eBooks that had been on the market for years.

No matter what your personal reading preference might be, your readers may want something different. And chances are, they are going to want a print copy of your book.

eBooks are real books...
One of my pet peeves is when people say they only read "real books." Usually, they say it with this sneer and a tone that somehow anything self-published is

actually covered in germs. Those people aren't my audience, but still their words were selected without any thought and you will undoubtedly come across them as an author.

eBooks are real books. They are real because your eyes can read them. Print books are real books too, but eBooks are no less real than print books. What these lazy, sneering, passersby mean is that they prefer to read printed books. But they don't know the meaning of basic words, so don't sweat their opinion too much.

If it looks like a duck…
Having your books only available in eBook format screams amateur. There are many ways to bring other formats to life without material cost (I will cover this in Chapter 4). Don't let the perceived cost hold you back.

In a time when a consumer likely can't tell the difference between a self-published book and a traditionally published book, you are telling them that you are a novice by only having your books available as an eBook. If your favorite author of all time has their book out in hardcover, paperback, eBook, and audiobook, you're not surprised because they are an established commodity. When you have your book in all formats, you are signaling that as well. Having your book out as an eBook is critically important in 2020. Having your book ONLY available as an eBook is a mistake.

When you publish your book in multiple formats, I suggest that you read through and edit for eBook first and then modify it for print as needed. In your eBook, you can have a hotlink to your bibliography sources or lead magnets (items that you offer for free to gain email subscriptions). You are required to have a linkable table of contents in your eBook by all the major platforms, but you can also link within the book any time you reference a previous chapter. You have more options with an eBook.

But you also have to make sure your book will still read well in an eBook format. If you have large images that you plan to include, will they still look good on a tiny smartphone screen? Are you planning to use fancy drop caps? Those usually look wonky in eBooks, so I would suggest not including them. (NOTE: some formatting software will include the drop caps, but I have seen these display weird in different eReader apps. I would suggest foregoing this option altogether for your eBook).

The most common types of eBooks are converted into ePub and Mobi file types. Mobi is short for Mobipocket and is specific to Amazon and its Kindle device. ePub file types can be used by other eReaders and eReading apps. Later in this book, I will discuss how you can take your finished manuscript and either upload it directly to a platform or have it converted on one platform and use that file elsewhere.

Advantages of Publishing as an eBook:

- You can get your book up and start selling it quickly.
- There are no print costs associated with each sale, only the split you have with your retailer.
- You can edit and update your manuscript as needed.

Disadvantages of Publishing as an eBook:

- As with all technology, there will be glitches you need to troubleshoot from time to time.
- It is easier for a scammer to pirate your work in this format (but this is very unlikely for first-time authors).
- There are multiple digital formats to manage for eBooks (ePub, Mobipocket, etc.)

Editable PDF

I was originally not going to mention this format as it is a subset of the eBook format. However, there are upcoming trends in self-publishing that are making editable PDFs more popular. Many online side-hustlers have seen the benefit of selling editable PDFs on websites like Etsy. These can be budget planners, grocery lists, monthly calendars, you name it. Printable PDFs that you can directly edit on your computer are a great way to make money and help people get organized. Many authors will even leverage these PDFs as part of their lead generation strategy to market their books.

With the increase in notebooks and journals by self-publishers, many authors are looking to release notebooks of their own. And the one thing they look to add on is another format. If you can sell a hardcover notebook or journal, why not also sell the editable PDF version?

For starters, as of Fuary 2020, not all publishing platforms will allow you to directly sell editable PDFs. Amazon is one of them. I know several authors who opt to sell these directly on their website instead. This requires a point of sale plugin for their website and some security measures to ensure the user can download the PDF again if they lose the file while preventing them from sharing it with others.

My recommendation is that if you want to sell your book as an editable PDF that you do a lot of research before proceeding. If your book is intended to be a workbook that people fill in, the best option may be a printed book. Adding an editable PDF will increase the complexity for you while adding a potential convenience to the reader. If you get one request for the editable PDF, make a note of it. Two, three, okay keep making notes. My caution is to not jump on this idea unless you know there is a real demand for it.

Advantages of Publishing as an Editable PDF
- Join in on the current trend as more consumers want to only interact with content digitally.

- Add an interactive element to the content you provide.

- Start to get feedback on what people do/do not like.

Disadvantages of Publishing as an Editable PDF

- As of January 2020, you can't sell these on Amazon and other large self-publishing platforms.

- You have to find a way to make sure the file isn't shared to those who haven't purchased it.

- To sell on your own website will require additional plugins and security.

Print - Paperback

In terms of getting your book to reach the most people, I see paperback as your best option. According to a Pew Research study, 37% of US adults say they will ONLY read print books. Another 28% say they will read either print or digital. Readers are familiar with this format. There is no chance the battery is going to die on their paperback just as the villain is about to be revealed. They can read it and physically pass it on to a friend without having to read intricate terms and conditions for lending the book out. They can put it on their shelf and take it down whenever they would like. It can be wrapped up with a bow and given as a gift for any major holiday or celebration.

Speaking from my personal experience, I will always have a paperback version of my books moving forward.

After stubbornly refusing to include this format for three years because I thought I could single-handedly save all the trees, I see now that this is the most popular format of all the books that I have sold.

In today's publishing world, you have many great options available to you as a self-published author. With the dawn of print-on-demand publishing, you can sell a printed copy of your book to readers without any up-front costs. Historically you would have to do a large bulk order of your book (offset printing) and then sell them out of your garage or spare room. With print-on-demand, the publishing platform has the information for your book. When someone clicks "buy," they print a copy and send it to the customer. This saves you the cost of the large order, warehousing, and shipping. But you will pay a bit more per book because you aren't realizing economies of scale. The cost of the book is deducted from the price that the consumer pays by your print-on-demand publishing platform.

Paperback books tend to be less expensive to produce than hardcover books, but you can still charge more for them than an eBook. This should give you a sweet spot in terms of the royalties you can realize with this format.

If you are just getting started and are looking for a proof of concept, eBooks may be the easiest way to get your book out on the market. But you may start to hear those requests for a tangible book quickly. Be ready to put your book out into paperback so that you can strike while the iron is hot.

When you are translating your manuscript from an eBook to any print medium (both paperback and hardcover), you will need to check that any hot-links that you have included are removed from the text (so that the lighter text font and underlined text styling go away) and ensure that this reference is included in your bibliography. This is more common in non-fiction books than in fiction, but it is critical to make sure that you don't have digital elements in your print book. I can poke at the book all I want; the link is never going to open.

Advantages of Publishing as a Paperback

- This remains the most popular format for readers.
- With print-on-demand (POD) services, you don't have to manage inventory.
- You get to actually hold your book!

Disadvantages of Publishing as a Paperback

- Once something is printed, it can't be unprinted. Errors will live forever in print.
- Even if the retailer damages the book in transit or has shipping issues, readers and reviewers will associate it with YOU.
- The cost to print and ship will cut into your margin.

Print - Hardcover

In traditional publishing, the standard strategy is to release the hardcover version of a book first as this has the highest price and the largest margin for the publishing company. The readers who really want the book will still buy it in this format. Once those sales trickle, then traditional publishers will release the book in other formats. There was also a stigma around paperback books for decades because they were seen as low-brow. There are still some readers who view paperback books this way, but I wouldn't spend too much time worrying about this specific subset of readers. More traditional publishers are now moving to the model where all formats are available on release, but they have been slower to adopt this strategy than independent authors.

What I will say is that for how expensive they are to produce, and therefore how expensive they are to sell, people still buy hardcover books. Some people prefer the feel and the weight of them. Some people like that the dust covers can double as bookmarks. In general, libraries like them because they can withstand more wear and tear over a paperback book. (We'll get your book into a library in Chapter 3).

I have seen this format sell well for my clients and my own books. I am still surprised every time someone buys the same book at a higher cost when they could get it for a fraction of the cost in digital format.

There are not as many great print-on-demand options for self-publishing authors when it comes to hardcover books, but they do exist. I would suggest that if you plan to release a series of fiction books, that you consider printing them in hardcover. People who are fans of your series may want to collect all of the hardcovers, and you then have the option to release a box set. I won't be going into the box-set strategy in this book because that isn't applicable for first-time authors. But it is something to keep in mind for your future writing.

Advantages of Publishing as a Hardcover
- Still a popular format for many readers.
- Books hold up better to wear and tear which is a plus for libraries.
- You get to actually hold your book!

Disadvantages of Publishing as a Hardcover
- There are added design decisions required for the book itself as well as the cover jacket.
- There are limited print-on-demand options for self-publishers.
- The cost to print and ship will cut into your margin.

Audiobook

I am only going to touch on audiobooks briefly in this

section. There is an entire book that I could write, and likely will, just about this format and how to create these for your catalog of books.

What I want you to think about at this stage is: how it will be adapted to audiobook? Is this a format you need? I think so. New reports come out each month showing the growth in demand for audio content. Be it podcasts or audiobooks, people want to be able to listen to something on their commutes, on their morning runs, or as they clean the house.

Reasons you may elect to not produce an audiobook out the gate could certainly be your resources: both financial and time-based.

However, if you have decided that you will have your book available in an audiobook format, you need to re-read through your book (yes, again) as though it was an audio script. In fact, you should click "Save As" and create a new version of your manuscript that is just for audio. Then you can add in commas and other breaks into the text that are not grammatically correct, but that will instruct your narrator to pause or change their inflection. Also, you may have visuals in your book (this could be graphs and charts in non-fiction or a clue or note in fiction) that would not be visible to the audiobook listener. You will need to add in text or modify it to get the same point across to your listener.

Advantages of Publishing as an Audiobook

● The format is growing in popularity for book consumers.

● The right narrator can bring your book to life.

● This is another method for readers to find your book.

Disadvantages of Publishing as an Audiobook

● Audio production and development are costly.

● The sound and editing quality will be closely scrutinized.

● You will need to remove or amend passages that assume the person is reading with their eyes.

At this point you should already have in your mind what formats you want to make your book available in. Write them down and rank them in order of importance to you and your vision. It is ideal to launch with each format ready to go, but if you find that you are running short on time and don't want to rush, you can always release in one format and release more as you go.

Now that you have your list of formats, you can start to work on the editing process. Remember these different formats as you and your editor read through the manuscript. Let's dive into those edits.

Chapter 2:

How do I Edit my Book?

"I have rewritten—often several times—every word I have ever published. My pencils outlast their erasers." —*Vladimir Nabokov, Speak, Memory, 1966*

Editing is a major component of writing. Once one draft is finished, it is time to start revising the next. This could go on for an infinite amount of time. Eventually, you will reach a point where you will say that your book is "good to go." Editing is not erasing all mistakes; it is erasing as many as you can. There is a certain amount of imperfection that comes with a human writing a book, a human editing the book, and a human doing a final sweep on the book. Even with the rise of AI and digital editing software, we can't rely on them for everything. Errors are found in books by the most popular authors. While readers may glance over a minimal amount, too many can result in poor reviews and lower sales.

Below are my key tips to successfully edit your book.

Self-edits

Self-editing is important in the process. However, you can't always view your work objectively, which is why you will bring in a third party. I recommend doing self-edits on the initial manuscript and at the very end of your process as well.

You should do at least two rounds of self-editing before you send your manuscript off to an editor. You may have been editing as you wrote the manuscript. This can happen when you use time dedicated to writing for re-reading your work instead.

As you do this edit, you should be looking for consistency and errors. By consistency I mean, does your main character spell their name John or Jon and is it shown in the same way every time they are referenced? Do you quote a statistic in two chapters with the same reference? Consistency is key for a smooth reading experience. Errors can be typos, grammatical issues, passive-voice, or plotlines that you thought you had removed, but are still referenced in the text.

For my process, I highlight each character's name, referenced location, and any words relating to specific dates and times in yellow. When I do my first read-through, these items stick out to me and I know I need to check for consistency. If I see any spelling or detail changes, I make a task in Asana (a free digital project management software). Then I know I need to go through and search for all references to this word or detail and make sure they are consistent in my final sweep.

After all the editing is done by my editors, I do another self-edit before hitting "publish." This self-edit usually involves me reading the book out loud with someone watching over my shoulder. That someone is usually my amazingly patient husband. I've picked up this tip from several authors along the way and I have found reading the book aloud helps me on several levels. I can catch any errors or missing words, get a feel for the flow, and practice for when I narrate the audiobook. I can hear if I use the same word too many times or if character names are too similar. Having someone look over my shoulder helps to make sure I don't read what isn't there. This happens. Our brains complete sentences that are missing words. Having someone read along as you narrate can prevent this. Because I don't want to miss any details, I break up my self-editing sessions into 30-minute increments so that my focus stays sharp.

In all of my self-edits, I am hyper-aware of everything

that I do wrong. I know my weaknesses are commas. When I do my second self-edit, I am critical of every comma use. I have been improving with each book that I publish, but I still know this needs my attention.

Take a few moments to reflect on your weaknesses. Do you have long, rambling sentences? Do you tend to give all your characters very similar names? Did you decide mid-story that you wanted to change the setting from New York to Los Angeles? Have you used the same statistic three times in one chapter? Use your first self-edit to focus on these known weaknesses to weed out as many as possible. You'll catch more on the second self-edit, but you will be able to see the other underlying errors better.

You know yourself better than your editor. As you work together on this book, and hopefully more, you will be able to learn what other areas you may need to focus on. But remember, your editor is human too. The way I have explained things to clients is that if my manuscript has 1,000 issues and my editor catches 90% of them, that is a great revision on their part. But 100 issues remain in the book. If I can do a self-edit and catch half of my issues and then the editor steps in, I would bet they would be able to catch more than 90% of the remaining issues. The cleaner your manuscript is by the time it lands with your editor, the more effective they can be in providing value to you.

Picking an Editor

You may (or may not) be surprised to learn that for my first book, I didn't hire an editor. I know, I committed cardinal sin #1 of being an author. But I was new and had limited funds to work with. Now you get the benefit of learning from my mistakes.

I did have someone proof my book though, she is my mother-in-law. Depending on your relationship with your in-laws you may think that this meant I got a really easy review or a really harsh one. The truth lies somewhere in between. My mother-in-law is a retired second grade teacher and an avid reader. We love to talk books together. She is a very sweet person and is usually the first in her book club to give a book a 4- or 5-star rating on Goodreads. She has told me in the past that she thinks some of the other members of her book club are too harsh. Or she doesn't like it when someone recommends a book with excessive swearing. Over the years that I knew her before I was ready to have someone take a look at my first novel, *Nailbiters*, I realized that she was just the person I needed. I was still stinging from the rejections of the traditional publishing world. I wanted to hear criticisms privately from someone I trusted and not from a troll in my reviews.

So, she read the book and sent back some thoughts on what wasn't clear, what punctuation rules I was mixing up, and what my options were for correcting it. I made the changes and sent it back. I told my husband that I was shocked she didn't have more to say, maybe I wasn't too bad after all. He read between the lines and sent her a text telling her I needed to hear the good, bad, and ugly from her and not random strangers on the internet. She sent back A LOT of red. While *Nailbiters* is far from perfect, I received honest and critical feedback from someone whose opinion I respected. She told me which sections she thought different people in her book club would love or hate. She caught stray commas and helped me to make my first book legible. She is still the first person outside my household who reads each of my books.

The purpose of telling you this is to say that it is OK for you to get feedback from someone you know. Yes, a friend or family member may tell you in a caring way, but they are still telling you what needs fixed. I have grown as an author, she has grown as an editor, and we both have learned so much along the way.

The first big takeaway that I want you to know about picking an editor is that you have to feel comfortable with this person. This person will tell you (and should tell you) if something isn't working or doesn't make sense. They will put red lines through entire patches of dialog that you thought were perfect.

Now that you know my first editorial experience and

that the biggest priority with your editor is the ability to have open communication and receive feedback, here are the nuts and bolts of editors. Keep in mind that ultimately, you know your book and can determine which feedback to incorporate. Let's get started with the bones and structure of your book:

Types of Editors - Developmental

When I started out writing, I thought all editors were the same. The person who would cross out entire plot points was also the person who would correct my colon and semicolon use. Not true at all.

There are different types of editors: developmental and copy. Within those two main categories, some editors specialize in different genres and mediums. You need to find the right one for you and your book.

What Developmental Editors Do

Developmental editors look at the manuscript as a whole and give you feedback about how the narrative fits together. Whether you are writing fiction or non-fiction, there is a narrative arc to your book (or there should be). The developmental editor will point out what isn't clear, what might need to be reordered or better explained. They will call out if you are glossing over something that may be endemic to your niche. They will tell you what you need to rework in terms of the big picture.

This is why you want to bring in developmental editors early on in the process. I would recommend working with your developmental editor after the first draft is complete. Because they are providing a specialized look at your manuscript that cannot be outsourced, even to the most enhanced AI program, developmental editors tend to charge more for their time. In the books that I have helped others publish, the developmental editor can take up to 6 weeks with the book (although I have seen them send back their notes sooner). When the developmental editor is working on the book, you as the author should not be fiddling around with it. You should also not pester them. If they provided a clear timeline of when to expect to hear from them and that date has come and gone, definitely reach out. Otherwise, let them do their work.

After the first edits come back, you as the author will go through the editorial letter and make any suggested changes as you see fit. The developmental editors that I have worked with have all been very clear that their opinions are just that, opinions. The author is free to take or leave them. This is the sign of a good editor. After the revisions are made, the manuscript usually goes back to the developmental editor for one more read through to make sure the author understood what was communicated. If you aren't sure, schedule a call to talk through their recommendations. As you work with the same developmental editor multiple times you may find that email communication gets easier and easier. I always like to talk through any comments to make sure everyone is on the same page. (Book puns!)

You may read this and think, "yeah, my budget barely fits a copy editor. I don't think I can afford two rounds with a developmental editor." If this is the case, you can rely on Beta Readers for help. There are Beta Readers out there that hire out their services for feedback on a book, but others will do this for free if they are part of a Beta Reading circle or are part of your personal network. However, if you don't have the budget for an experienced developmental editor, you probably won't be able to afford a paid Beta Reader. Instead make a list of people in your life who meet these conditions:

- They read books on a regular basis
- They generally like your genre or topic
- They are opinionated or at least know how to give critical feedback

All three of these conditions are important. The first two will mimic the ideal audience for your book: people who read books in your genre. The third condition is important because you need critical feedback. You need your opinionated friend Nancy to tell you exactly where in the story you lost her interest. You need your cousin Barry who knows everything about everything to tell you when in your argument you glossed over some important points.

When you send your manuscript off to Beta Readers, I would strongly suggest that you put a watermark on the document. This watermark can say "Proof" or "Beta Review" or "Confidential." I will try to put the Beta Reader's name on the watermark when it is feasible. This provides you with some security for the book and it makes that person feel special to see their name on the watermark. I would also suggest that you request feedback to be sent back by a specific date. This way you don't get feedback on the book a year after you publish it. This also gives you a chance to pool the feedback. You can't please everyone. If you get feedback from Nancy first you may start to take action on her edits. But then Barry sends his feedback and you rewrite again based on that. With your Beta Readers, you are looking for larger trends. Did everyone say that one plot point was unclear? Then it's unclear. Did one person say that they didn't like a character name because it happens to be the name of their ex-boyfriend? That suggestion may not make your list of required edits. I have known authors who rewrote their books multiple times to appease an individual Beta Reader. They spent years redoing their work to try and make everyone happy.

Remember, at the end of the day, you have to be happy with the end result.

Here are some questions to ask when evaluating a developmental editor:

• **What kinds of books do you prefer to edit?** – you want to make sure that they have experience working with books in your genre.

• **What is your rate?** – make sure that you have an understanding of everything included and how many rounds of edits this covers. If you have to pay that rate for both rounds then it is really double that cost.

• **What is your usual process?** – this helps you discover what you can expect. You can also gauge their experience level. If they only tell you one step out, they may be trying to launch their editing services and may only know the next step in the process. This isn't good or bad. If you are trying to save, you may be able to negotiate a lower rate with someone who is just starting out. If they are charging top dollar, you want to know they have experience.

Types of Editors - Copy Editing

Copy editing is the type of editing that most people think of when they hear an author refer to this process. Copy editing goes by many names: line editing, proofreading, nit-picking. This is when the typos get taken out. The "theirs" and "there's" and "they'res" sorted out. The extra commas and missing question marks. This is the grammar and spelling portion of editing the book. It is just as tedious for the editor to go through the manuscript as it is for the author to make the edits.

When I am looking through copy edits, I prefer to work in a Microsoft Word document or a Google Doc with tracked changes that I can accept or reject to make the process easier.

I have found that readers will be more critical of a grammatical error or a typo than they will with plot issues or questions left unresolved. I have even heard of some readers spotting a typo, slamming the book shut, and giving it a 1-star review, even if they were loving the story up until that point. Some people are very particular when it comes to reading a perfect book. I tend to smile when I catch a typo, especially if it is from a famous author. **We all make mistakes.** But ideally, we do want to keep them to a minimum in our published werks. (Haha okay, that one was intentional).

For those looking to hire a professional copy editor, their rates should be lower than the developmental editor. Some authors are in the habit of using two copy editors. If you decide to do this, I would suggest having the first do their edit, review their feedback, make revisions, and then send it to the second editor. This way you won't have to try and marry the two documents and decipher competing edits.

Again, if you find that a professional editor is out of your budget for your first book, you can always ask friends and family members to help. We all have at least one person in our circle who is a "grammarist."

Someone who knows all of the rules and is happy to correct any grammatical issues because it just hurts their brain when they see them. If they love to read, they may do it at no cost. But you may still want to treat them to dinner or provide another gift to show your appreciation.

As you send out your ARCs (Advance Reader Copies) of your book, you can let your team know to send over any issues if they find them. (I discuss ARCs and building a Street Team in my regular videos that you can find on AuthorYourAmbition.com/Videos and in *Book Marketing for the First-Time Author*.) I find that advance readers feel a sense of ownership and report typos right away. They feel included in the process and want to help. Thankfully, by the time it gets to that stage the errors are few and far between.

When I format the book after all edits are done, I still run each paragraph through Grammarly as well. I can do this with their free version and by this point in the process I don't find many edits, but there are always one or two that can be weeded out. There are many benefits to using editing software like Grammarly or built-in editors in your word processor. But they are not perfect, so don't rely on them 100%.

The same questions that you would ask a developmental editor will apply when you are screening a copy editor. You want to make sure they have experience in your genre, they are upfront about their pricing, and they are going to work with you through the process.

Pricing Structures for Editors

When you are looking to hire an editor, either developmental or copy, you will first need to look at their pricing structure.

There are three pricing structures that I have seen editors advertise:
- Flat rate
- Word rate
- Hourly rate

I have noticed that only novice or beginner editors use flat rates. No matter how long your manuscript is, they charge one fee. You could come out way ahead in this regard, or you could grossly overpay. But you know the total cost upfront. This could be a great way for you to get a good deal for your editing services. Just because someone is new to this, doesn't mean they won't do a good job. But be sure to ask them to review a sample chapter first so you can see how you will work together and what they can catch.

Most of the editors I have worked with charge a rate based on the number of words. If the book is 70,000 words and the editor charges $0.02/word that works out to $1,400 for the editing fee. This is a fair deal for the editor because their rate is based on the volume of work they are editing.

Then I have seen editors who operate on an hourly rate they back into based on how many words they can edit in a given hour. In the word rate and hourly rate charges, the editor should ask for your word count upfront. You should also be clear about the content. I have worked on books that were math-heavy. I asked the editor if they felt comfortable editing this content as well. The more you communicate at the outset, the better off you will both be as you work together.

Look for Editors Who Ask:

When you set out to look for a professional editor, I would recommend asking other authors which editors they have worked with and had a good experience with. Be sure to ask authors in your genre so the editor is experienced with your topic.

When I first started my self-publishing journey, I didn't know any other authors. Thankfully there are amazing groups on Facebook and other social platforms you can connect with. I have found that most of these groups are welcoming and helpful.

Recommendations are a great place to start, but be sure to do your own due diligence. While you now know to ask about their experience, the books they usually work with, and their rates, you should look for an editor who knows to ask these questions:

• **Can I see a sample chapter so I can give you an estimate for the current level of editing the manuscript will need?** Then I can better estimate my time and give you a more accurate price. This demonstrates they have experience in editing and they know what types of books they want to work on. It can help them to determine how much time this project will take and if they can work you into their schedule.

• **Can you pay half as a down payment?** This tells you they understand the risk on both sides. You are trusting them with your book baby. You are trusting they will do the work they say they will do. They are telling you they trust you will pay them the rest of the fee once their work is done.

• **How do you prefer to work together? Via email, calls, text?** Someone who has the experience to ask how you prefer to communicate has done this before. It also shows they want to work together and ensure a smooth process.

Now you are all set to send off your manuscript and have it ripped to pieces, I mean, improved and polished so you put your best foot forward. Once you find your developmental and copy editor, send your book out and prepare to make edits as they come back to you. While you wait for revisions to be sent, you can work on setting up the technical details for self-publishing.

Chapter 3:

What are the Technical Details to Keep Track of?

The great thing about publishing is that there are some really antiquated processes to go through where you find yourself in a bit of a catch-22. Did I say great? I meant annoying. But thankfully, I've dealt with these annoying processes enough that I know what I am doing now and can make this easier for you.

The first time I went through the process of getting my book recognized by the Library of Congress and assigning an ISBN, I was a nervous wreck. These were official government forms that I was filling out. This information would go on the permanent record for my books.

Below are the details that were extremely hard for me to find when I was starting. I've put them all together for you here.

Before you take the time to read this section, you first need to answer several questions about your goals:

• Do you want your book available in your local public library and thousands of other libraries across the country?

• Do you want your book to be on bookshelves at local bookstores or even big box stores?

• How big is your dream for the book?

• Are you looking for the simplest or lowest-cost solution?

When I started out, I was very optimistic about how *Nailbiters* would do. But I wasn't completely delusional. I knew it would be a tough start, but I had read several books on positive visualization. I thought that I needed to be realistic about how the book would sell, but that I needed to be prepared for success. I made decisions for my book based on my long-term plans and goals.

The reason that you need to think long-term is that it will determine if you register for a Publisher Control Number (PCN) and Library of Congress Control Number (LCCN). It will also determine if you own your International Standard Book Number (ISBN) and if you purchase a barcode for your book.

In my case, I wanted my books to be available in libraries and I wanted to have full control of my work. That meant I needed a PCN, LCCN, and ISBNs. I'll explain the process for each of these below.

CIP and PCN

For your book to be available in a local library, it needs to have a Library of Congress Control Number (LCCN). Before you can get one of those, you need a Publisher Control Number (PCN). Both of these are available for FREE through the Library of Congress Cataloging in Publication (CIP) program. As a government program, they LOVE their acronyms. The nice thing about each of these programs is they are FREE. The only thing it will cost you is some time. That is why you need to plan ahead.

In the Spring of 2019, the PCN and CIP programs were merged and the website to apply to CIP was upgraded. It looks much better and is more user-friendly. To apply to join the CIP program, you will need to create a login on the portal. For anyone who had a PCN as a self-published author before the changeover, you will need to sign up anew through the updated website.

Because an actual human working for the government will review your application, it can take a while to get a response. To be safe, go through this process 6 weeks before publication. When I first applied it took a week for me to get a response. As I have applied for my clients, it has taken a few days. But, don't assume anything when it comes to these applications. Plan ahead. Be sure to complete the application as thoroughly as possible to ensure that it is approved the first time around.

LCCN

Once you are set up with a login to the CIP program, you can apply for your LCCN. Your book, no matter what format, will have the same LCCN. If you have your book available as an eBook, paperback, and hardcover, you will have just one LCCN to apply to all formats. However, when you apply for the LCCN you will need to indicate the ISBNs associated with your title. The thing is, when you assign your ISBN, you are asked for the LCCN.

Let's jump ahead to ISBNs to make sure we follow this intricate loop.

ISBN

Remember back in Chapter 1 when I went into all that detail about the book formats? All of that information comes into play here.

Your ISBN is the Social Security number for your

book. It is the identifying number that will be used by all retailers to look up the title and version. It is the most important piece of information about your book that you will have to enter over and over again.

Your ISBN meta-data carries all kinds of information about your book: the language, the publication year, the publisher, the format, etc. When you purchase and assign your ISBNs you are effectively the parent on this book birth certificate. When you receive a "free" ISBN from any service, they are the parent. When you control your ISBN, you can elect to publish your book through any platform. If you find soaring success and a traditional publisher or movie studio wants to do business with you, there are no impediments. When someone else owns your ISBN, you have an added layer of complexity to deal with.

One of the reasons I always stress owning your ISBNs is that you are in control of your book. Also, if someone else is assigning you an ISBN, you won't know it in time to apply for your LCCN to have it listed on your copyright page.

For each version of your book, you will need an individual ISBN. In the example above where you have an eBook, paperback, and hardcover formats of your book (three versions) you will need three ISBNs.

Once you assign an ISBN to a given title and format, you can't change it. Take your time and pay attention to the details.

United States - Bowker

In the United States, you can purchase ISBNs individually or in bundles from Bowker. Because you can go through multiple ISBNs for 1 title, I recommend starting with the 10-pack bundle. Some clients I have worked with say that they want to create a workbook or a journal where the intent is for someone to hold the book and write in it. They decided to purchase just 1 ISBN.

As of January 2020, the cost for 1 ISBN through Bowker is $125. The cost for the 10-pack is $295. The cost for the 100-pack is $575. There are economies of scale with the bundles. Because of this, if you plan to only ever write 1 book and release it in 1 format, get 1 ISBN. If you think your book will be in more than 1 format and that you might have more than 1 book to write, get the 10-pack.

When you are ready to apply for your LCCN and have your ISBN purchased, have both webpages set up on different tabs or windows on your computer. Fill out the information for your LCCN until you get to the part where you need to enter the ISBN. Then switch over to Bowker and click on an available ISBN under "My Identifiers." Start to fill out the information for your ISBN. Because you will not know your LCCN, leave that blank. You may not have your cover image yet; you can leave that blank. The important thing here is for anything you don't know, leave it blank. You can go back in and add information later, but you will not be able to change the required fields such as format and title.

Once you have all of the information available filled out for your ISBN, copy the number and switch back to the LCCN application. Enter the ISBN and proceed. You will get a confirmation email from the Library of Congress that your LCCN application has been received and then another communication once it has been assigned.

I strongly suggest that you start to keep track of these important details all in one place. Because I have multiple books, I keep track of all these details on a spreadsheet so I know the exact publication date, ISBN, LCCN, and ASIN for every book. (The ASIN is the product code for Amazon. We will cover all things Amazon in Chapter 4.) Since this is your first book, you can keep track of them on one sheet of paper. I have created a "Book Birth Certificate" for authors to keep these details in one place. Visit **AuthorYourAmbition.com/Book-Birth-Certificate/** to claim yours today.

Outside the United States
For those of you who live outside the United States, you probably just read the last section thinking that

none of this information applies to you. Most of it does. You still need 1 ISBN for every format you publish. You still need to be careful as you complete this information because once it is assigned you cannot change the details.

The good news is that you may not have to worry about ISBN costs because Canadian and UK authors can get their ISBNs for FREE. Look up the specific requirements for your country by doing an internet search for: "[YOUR COUNTRY] + ISBN".

Barcodes

I'm sure by this point in your life, you have noticed the weird lines on the back of every package you've ever purchased in a store. Barcodes make point of sale easy for retailers. They contain lots of information about the item; including the price and help retailers to maintain accurate inventory.

Depending on your vision and goals for your book you may or may not need a barcode. If you plan to only publish an eBook, you don't need a barcode. No physical item will ever pass over a barcode scanner. You can skip this section.

If you plan to sell print copies of your book through a print-on-demand service, you will need to carefully read their policies on barcodes. For example, Amazon KDP will provide a barcode for any paperbacks that they print, but you can still bring your own. IngramSpark requires that authors provide cover art with the barcode included.

You may read that and think, 'I'll just go with Amazon KDP to save myself the inconvenience.' I did this for my third book, *Enemies of Peace*, the first book I decided to publish with a paperback edition. (I have since gone back and released the first two in paperback as well.) I will go into more detail about Amazon KDP later, but what you need to know for now is that the barcode that they provide contains all of the information except for the price. This is because you as the author will be able to change the price at any time. Amazon doesn't want to have to keep providing you with new barcodes every time you change the price or get stuck with inventory they can't use.

Did you catch that? If you change the price of your book, you need a new barcode. To prevent this, you can purchase a barcode for yourself without the price listed. For authors in the United States, you would also purchase the barcode from Bowker. You need to be very careful when filling out the information because once it is set, it cannot be changed without having to purchase another. Electing to buy a barcode without any price information probably sounds like the best route right about now.

But brick and mortar retailers don't want to stock books where the barcode doesn't have the price information. They would have to manually set the price in their point of sale system to be able to stock the book. Then they may still have to check the price at checkout. If your dream is to walk into your local bookstore and see your book on the shelves, you are going to need to publish with a barcode that has your price on it.

This is a double-edged sword as we will see when we cover pricing later. If you want to offer a lower price, you need a new barcode. If you want to increase the price, you need a new barcode. If the retailer decides they want to offer a discount, they just update the information in their point of sale system, no new barcode needed. It adds a layer of complexity and cost for independent authors. However, it is a critical step if you want a brick and mortar retailer to stock your book.

Copyright Page

It's worth noting here, that I am not a lawyer. I have no official degree or license that gives me any authority to talk about copyright law and you should do your own research and contact a lawyer for assistance with your copyright page.

As with everything else I have learned over the years, my copyright pages have evolved with my books. I almost forgot to include a copyright page in my first book. A rookie mistake.

Now I have a template that I use for each of my books. I have added to this and edited it based on the research I did online. I did an internet search for: "fiction copyright page template." I switched out the information I needed and moved on.

You know you are a real-life professional author when you genuinely enjoy scoping out copyright pages. As an avid reader, I started to look at what other authors included in their books. I incorporated clauses that I thought were useful, such as the "all persons fictitious" disclaimer that I now include for all of my fiction books. As an author, we know to not plagiarize, but there are truly only so many ways you can say "no unauthorized copies" or "all rights reserved." It is okay to have that same wording on your copyright page.

Your copyright page should go immediately after your title page. It's right at the front so that anyone can easily find it.

Elements of your copyright page:
- **Copyright Mark** © - This is your copyright mark and year. I have seen book templates that include just this. While this checks the box, it is not anywhere near sufficient.

- **All Rights Reserved** - This is the paragraph that expressly states that all rights regarding your copyright are reserved by you, the publisher. It prohibits any duplications or reproduction. Because you are not allowing any unauthorized copies, you need to provide a means for someone to reach out to obtain authorization. This can be an email address or physical address. Since you need to provide a physical address on the copyright page, you might as well just include it once. Some authors will set up a P.O. Box for this so they can keep their physical address private and they don't have to update it every time they move.

This is the exact copy that I have used for my books: *"All rights reserved. No part of this publication may be reproduced, distributed, or transmitted in any form or by any means, including photocopying, recording, or other electronic or mechanical methods, without the prior written permission of the publisher, except in the case of brief quotations embodied in critical reviews and certain other noncommercial uses permitted by copyright law. For permission requests, write to the publisher, addressed "Attention: Permissions Coordinator," at the address below."*

- **ISBN and LCCN** - You need to include these important numbers. You should modify your copyright page for each format so the ISBN is specific to that format. The ISBN listed on your eBook copyright page should be the one that you assigned for that format. The ISBN listed on your paperback copyright page should be the one that you assigned for that format. And so on.

- **Disclaimers** - For fiction books, I would recommend adding an "all persons fictitious" disclaimer. This says that you made all of your characters up and even though they may be described to look or act like a real-life person, they are not real. For non-fiction books you should include that you are not providing tax or legal advice and that the book is written for entertainment purposes only. This will not take the teeth out of the content of your book, but it will protect you should someone read your book, experience negative circumstances, and then decide to sue you. If you are writing something where you think that could reasonably happen, consult with an attorney on the disclaimer as well as the content of the book.

- **Design Credit** - This is where you can list your designer for the cover and any interior design. You should also provide photo credit here if your cover image has any photo elements.

- **Address & Website** - If you use the text I provided above, you will need to provide an address for any requests. Provide your website as well.

I have acquired this information over several years. As you do your research to publish your first book, this can all seem overwhelming, but it is important that you protect your work. You just spent how long writing and editing this book? You want to make sure it is protected and that you have control of your intellectual property.

There are experts in this field that you can learn from to dig deeper into this topic. Since you are reading this book, and therefore may appreciate learning from a book rather than another medium, I would recommend reading Helen Sedwick's *Self-Publisher's Legal Handbook.* I read this book as I was preparing to write down all of my years of knowledge for you. I was pleasantly surprised to see that I had been doing things right and that my years of taking the extra steps to protect my copyright had not been misled. Sedwick dives into more topics than I will cover in this book. Because she is a legal expert, and I am not, I would recommend that you consult her work for more detailed information on that topic.

After this chapter, you should be able to set up your book so that it is ready to be published. Next, we will cover the platforms where you can self-publish your book.

Chapter 4:

Where can I Publish my Book?

The biggest concern for every author is making sure people have access to buy their books. That means you need to sell through retailers. You could also sell it directly on your website, but how will people know to go to your website? The availability to list your title with current retailers is a huge benefit to authors.

Throughout this section, I am going to give you my first-hand experience with each of the following platforms:
- Amazon
- Google
- Smashwords

- StreetLib
- IngramSpark
- ACX
- Findaway Voices

Other platforms exist which I do not list here because they represent a small percentage of the market or offer a duplicate service to what I have already discussed. Before signing on with any platform, do your research on the most recent terms and conditions for that service as well as any up to date reviews.

I am going to walk you through several of the big factors when it comes to each of these platforms:
- Cost
- Set-Up Process
- Distribution and Reach
- Pros
- Cons

My aim here is to help you pick a platform, or multiple platforms, and feel confident in your choice. Once you start on this journey you are going to receive a lot of advertisements for new self-publishing platforms and deals. If you aren't confident in your publishing plan, you will spend a lot of extra effort doubting your choices, signing up for additional services, and taking time away from the thing you want to be doing: writing your next book.

Amazon Only Vs. Wide

Before getting into a discussion on all platforms, this is a good time to pause and take a look at two major strategies in the self-publishing space. Because Amazon offers special programs to authors who publish their books exclusively with their platform, many authors publish through the Amazon Only method. On the other side of the spectrum are those who want their book available on many platforms. Even if the Amazon exclusive programs would be helpful, they forego those opportunities to publish elsewhere. This is known as Going Wide.

There are many articles, podcasts, YouTube videos, and entire Facebook groups dedicated to these strategies and understanding what is best for you.

I know authors who are exclusive with Amazon. But Amazon is not their only source of income. Their book revenue is one pillar they added to an existing business of podcasting and writing blogs.

If you want to be an author and continue to write books and one day hope to live off of those royalties, then you should not be exclusive with one retailer. Imagine if a decade ago, I bragged that my book was exclusive with Borders? Or that you could only get it at Sears? Amazon has disrupted the retail book market and they have the greatest market share of all book sales, *for now*. But they will eventually be disrupted. And more to the point, not everyone gets their books from Amazon. Yes, many people do. But not everyone. What about those who read from their library? What about people in other countries who prefer a different online retailer or cannot easily access Amazon?

In the past year, my sales outside of the Amazon platform have grown to 50% of my annual book royalties. It took time to build this audience, but imagine if I had elected to only sell through Amazon. I may be missing out on half of my potential sales.

This is all to say that you should do your own research and understand the short-term and long-term implications of the decision to go Amazon Only or Publish Wide.

Amazon

How do I get my Book on Amazon?

Amazon occupies a unique place in publishing. Each time I speak with a new client I tend to have to explain the distinctions that exist within this mega-brand. Here are the three key things to keep in mind about Amazon and the book industry:

1. Amazon is first and foremost an online retailer. When they were founded in 1994 it primarily sold books. I remember that my mom pre-ordered *Harry*

Potter and the Goblet of Fire for me via Amazon so that it would be delivered to our house the day it was released. There was no risk of going into Barnes & Noble to find it had sold out at the midnight party. (I was also a total brat and begged her to let me go to the midnight release party with a lightning bolt drawn on my forehead because my best friend was going.)

2. Amazon has a self-publishing platform known as Kindle Direct Publishing (KDP). From this platform, anyone can upload their eBook or Paperback manuscript and sell directly on Amazon.com.

3. Amazon has a traditional publishing arm called Amazon Publishing. This arm operates much like any other traditional publisher. Their signed authors get the full benefit of the Amazon brand and marketing machine supporting their book.

The reason I take the time to explain all of this, is the first question I get from every client I work with is "how do I get my book on Amazon?"

There are many ways to accomplish this. I also tend to get questions after the book has been released about "updating the description on Amazon" or "updating the price on Amazon." If the book is distributed exclusively through KDP, this is a simple request. But if it is through an aggregator, a platform that publishes the book to multiple retailers at once, I always make sure to specify that any listing update will go through to all retailers. Because, believe it or not, Amazon is not the only place where people get their books. It is the largest online retailer, it is where most people get their books, but it is not the only place. As a writer, I am always looking for the most specific words in my books. As a publisher, I am always encouraging my clients, and I encourage you as well, to be specific in how you refer to Amazon. This will help you as you continue to focus on your strategy.

How can I Publish on Amazon Directly?

The better question to ask is, how can I publish on Amazon directly? The answer is Kindle Direct Publishing (KDP). This service title comes from Amazon's Kindle device and app. You can also publish your paperback books through this system.

When you publish through KDP, your book will be available on the Amazon platform for sale. Since Amazon is one of the largest retailers on the planet, this gets your book in front of a lot of readers.

Here are the highlights to consider when you are looking at publishing through KDP.

Cost

There is no cost to publish on KDP. If you upload your book and nothing sells, you don't pay a dime. Amazon will even offer a "free" ISBN. I recommend that you bring your own ISBN with you if you want to maintain full ownership of your work. This includes the ability to sell your book on platforms outside of Amazon. If you plan to publish books as an add-on to your existing business and don't plan to publish it outside the Amazon ecosystem, then you can just use their ISBN.

Amazon isn't letting you publish on their platform because they want to see authors succeed. They want a cut of the sales. There are a few avenues here for the royalty options:

eBooks
- You can elect to earn a 35% royalty on all sales
- You can elect to earn a 70% royalty on all sales

You might read this and think, *hmm why would anyone pick the 35% rate instead of the 70% rate?* Well, if you elect to charge less than $2.99 for your eBook, you have to pick the 35% royalty rate. Many self-published authors who are putting out their first book know that they need to be competitive with their pricing in order to attract new readers. Authors often want to offer their books at a discounted rate to drive demand. The number of reasons why an author will elect to charge less than $2.99 for their eBook is endless. No matter their strategy, if they charge less than $2.99 for their eBook, they have to take the lower royalty rate of 35%.

If you charge $2.99 or higher for your eBook you can elect to take the 35% royalty rate or the 70% royalty rate. I have not met any person who has picked the 35% rate when their eBooks are priced over $2.99.

Paperback
- You earn a 60% royalty
- You can elect to earn a royalty on the Expanded Distribution Network

The paperback royalties involve a little more math. Why? Because Amazon has to print and ship these; whereas, the eBooks arrive digitally in the users' Kindle. Your royalty is based on 60% of the list price, and then you subtract the print cost to see what you will earn. If it costs Amazon $3.72 to print your book, you want to set the list price at $10 or higher to ensure you make money on each sale. When you walk through the Paperback set-up you will see the estimated print price and Amazon will display an estimated royalty per book to make this easier for you to determine.

As an example, if I list my book for $11.99 and I sell one copy, Amazon will take 40% of the sale right away. I am left with $7.19. After subtracting the $3.72 cost to print, I am left with a $3.47 royalty on the sale of the book.

The other option I mentioned was their expanded distribution network. Just by the name alone, it sounds great. It seems to answer for the biggest problem with publishing on KDP: getting your book sold with other retailers. The program description gives this impression as well. However, brick and mortar retailers are getting hammered by Amazon. Most will not carry a book if it is printed in an Amazon facility.

The reality of expanded distribution is it allows 3rd party resellers to sell "new" or used copies of your book at any price they wish. If they bid up on your "buy" button on Amazon their price can become the default. I elected to join the expanded distribution network for my third novel, Enemies of Peace, my most successful book at the time of this printing. I made $0.40 after months of having it available through this option. I looked on my book's Amazon page and saw someone was trying to resell it for $40. My retail price at the time was $9.99. Needless to say, expanded distribution is not something I found success with. That doesn't mean you won't, but it helps to know what you are getting when you sign on for this network.

Set-Up Process

The process of setting up your KDP account is simple. First, go to kdp.amazon.com. If you are already signed into your Amazon account, you can log in with one click of a button. If you want to separate your personal shopping on Amazon from your publishing, you can create a second account. Some authors like to do this to keep personal and business separate, then it makes sense to have different accounts. (NOTE: Amazon is smart. It will see that you are logging in on the same computer, so you won't be able to circumvent their review policies with this tactic.)

On the first page of KDP, you will see your "Book Shelf." The process of creating a book is as simple as clicking on the big "+" on the page. Because KDP now offers both eBook and Print book options, you can create one format and then click "add Paperback" so that the two books are automatically linked.

As you go through the set-up process, you will fill in the information about your book. Note: You should only be completing this information once your book is done and ready to upload. I know some authors who fill this out, upload a rough draft, and set the release date for a few months in the future just so they have something up on the website. They figure the deadline will push them to make all of their edits on time. Some people thrive under this kind of pressure. But I've seen these authors on their release week, and they didn't appear to be thriving. They were stressed and nervous. So, just wait until you are completely ready to upload your book.

As you work through the set-up, you will be prompted to add the book title, description, keywords, ISBN, manuscript, cover art, and price. The set-up is easy to follow, and once you have the manuscript and cover art uploaded you will be able to see a digital proof of your book. ALWAYS review every page of the proof. For the few times that I have been uploading a revision and thought, "everything will be fine," it was not fine. You are publishing this book. Your name is on it. Look at every page of your preview.

Once you are done you will see a pop-up letting you know that your book will be vetted by someone at Amazon. I've never had any issues with my book not passing the vetting process. (I think this is because I always wait to upload to Amazon until after I get through the Smashwords AutoVetter, more on that later.) You will receive an email to confirm that your book has been submitted and then again once it is approved for sale.

The same goes for your paperback. In either case, it can take up to 72 hours for your book to be approved and listed on the site. This is why you should always plan ahead. For those who want to launch their pre-sale on a specific day, you're going to have to submit your book ahead of that date. In most cases, the book is approved within a few hours. However, if Amazon says it can take up to 72 hours, then plan for the full 72 hours.

Distribution & Reach

Through KDP, your book will be available on the Amazon platform for instant download (eBooks) and Print-On-Demand publishing for your paperback books.

Keep in mind that other aggregators that I will mention later can also publish your book into the Amazon ecosystem.

Kindle Unlimited/Kindle Select

One of the biggest benefits of publishing with Amazon through KDP is access to Amazon's advertising programs if you enroll in Kindle Select. Authors who are enrolled in Kindle Select can offer deals on their books, such as limited time offers with a special countdown clock. Their books are also part of the Kindle Unlimited subscription. Much like all other subscription services that you are familiar with, readers pay a monthly fee to Amazon and they can read as many books in Kindle Unlimited as they want. Authors are paid on a per-page-read model. This seems fair on its face. If you wrote an amazing book and readers keep going through your whole book, you make more than someone who wrote a dud.

The deal gets even better when you have a cache of books in a series. If I simply have to find out what happens to this character next, of course, I am going to read the next book and the next. Many voices in the independent and self-publishing space who talk about being "Kindle Millionaires" have done so through this program. Through a strategy of careful genre selection and a "rapid release" model, these authors have found success with Kindle Unlimited. eBooks that are available through Kindle Unlimited are still available for purchase on Amazon, so authors make a royalty on those direct sales as well.

One of the limitations of the Kindle Unlimited program is that payouts are fixed to an allocated pool of money. If 1 million pages are read in Month A, the pool of money is divided out based on that page count. If the page count doubles in Month B, but the pool of money stays the same, then the payout per page goes down.

You may think this isn't a deal-breaker. But, guess what is? Listing your book anywhere else. That's right, if your eBook is enrolled in Kindle Select, you must exclusively list it with Amazon. Because so many consumers make their purchases through Amazon, this may not seem like a bad deal to you. But if you want your local library to have a copy of your book, you would be violating this policy with Amazon. They remove violators from their system.

This is where the Amazon Only v. Publish Wide debate becomes an actual debate. If most of your royalties are going to come from Amazon anyway, why does it matter if you are exclusive with them? Well, what happens if Amazon faces a new competitor in the space and loses market share? What happens if more and more people are publishing to Kindle Select, and that pool of money doesn't grow? These are questions you have to answer for yourself.

When you upload your book to Amazon, you will see that you are already opted into Kindle Select. If you don't want to be in this program, you need to uncheck that box. If you want to be in the program, leave it checked, but now you are locked in for 90 days.

For my first two books, I elected to Publish Wide. I knew I wanted them at my local library, I knew I wanted them available to other online retailers. But over 70% of my sales were from Amazon after two years. When my third book, *Enemies of Peace*, was ready to release, I decided to give Kindle Select a try.

When I uploaded *Enemies of Peace*, I left the Kindle Select box checked and only made my book available in eBook and Paperback through Amazon. I didn't upload it anywhere else. As a reader, you could only read this book through Amazon. I saw that I was getting a thousand or so pages read through Kindle Unlimited each month. Not too bad. But then, the page views fell off. I renewed in Kindle Select four times, which is to say I didn't change my election in KDP for a year. But after a year, I was getting next to no royalties from Kindle Select. To be fair, I had shifted my focus to working with my clients and was barely able to write my fourth book, let alone market *Enemies of Peace*. I took *Enemies of Peace* out of Kindle Select and added it to other platforms. It is still one of my highest selling books and has done well on other retailers now that it is available there as well. (And remember, while

Amazon was my primary source of royalties for the first two years, it is now roughly 50%.)

Some authors elect to do a hybrid model where they are exclusive with Amazon and enroll in Kindle Select for the first 90 days and then publish their book Wide. But, how much excitement and buzz will you still be generating after that initial 90 days? That is another question you have to answer for yourself.

Pros
- Your book is available for sale on Amazon.
- Amazon gives you the option for a "free" ISBN.
  - I still suggest you purchase your own to maintain control.
- You can elect to participate in Kindle Select and Kindle Unlimited (KU).
- You can have both eBook and Paperback versions of your book available for sale.

Cons
- No hardcover option as of yet.
- Barcode on paperback has no fixed cost.
- Brick and mortar retailers won't carry books printed by Amazon.
  - Because of the barcodes.
  - Also, because they are killing brick and mortar retailers.

- Automatically opting you into KU.
  - ○ You have to select that you do not want to be included when you go through the set-up.
- No Paperback pre-order.
  - ○ You can do an eBook pre-order, but not for paperback.

Google

On to our next technology giant: Google! Just as there are Google Play Apps, Google Movies, and Google Music, there are Google Books. When I started on my self-publishing journey, Google was, surprisingly, not on my radar. Again, I had my blinders up, and I have learned things the hard way.

The great thing about having my books available through Google Play is that when I search for my name, all my books pop up now. The downside is that I've only recently started on this channel and have no reviews. It's a work in progress.

Here is what you need to know:

Cost
You can upload your manuscript to sell as an eBook without any cost to you. You will need to bring your own ISBN, but Google does not charge you to list your book on their site. Royalties vary between 52% and 70% in certain markets. The remainder of the sale will

go to Google.

Set-Up Process

Once you are approved to publish on Google Play, the set-up process is fairly easy.

Yes, you read that right. Approved. You need to apply to be a publisher on their platform. The application process is easy; start here: https://play.google.com/books/publish/u/0/. It took me a few minutes to fill out the application.

I waited almost a year after I applied to get approved. Once I was all clear, I uploaded my books and set the pricing. The process asks the same questions that Amazon and other self-publishing platforms do: title, description, categories, price, etc. The set-up form is very clear and easy to use.

Because my marketing time has been limited, I haven't dedicated much time to promoting that my books are available on Google Play. I plan to remedy this in the future. Even considering my lack of advertising, I have seen sales grow on this platform every month.

When you upload your eBook to Google, you will need to provide an ePub file. Because of this, I suggest that you upload your book with Smashwords first. Then you will have an ePub version to submit. I will discuss this service in just a few pages.

Distribution & Reach

The great thing about Google is its international reach. While some countries restrict the search engine, most use it regularly. When a reader in Austria asked me where they could buy my book that wasn't through Amazon, I told her that it was available on Google Play. She bought the book right away.

Pros

- Available on Google Play.
- Pops-up when you Google your name/pen name.
- Competitive royalties.

Cons

- The publisher interface isn't as easy to use for reporting.
  o I have to download reports to see details on which books were sold and at what royalty rate.
- This platform only supports eBooks.
- The delay in getting set-up due to the application and approval process.

Publishing Aggregators

Publishing Aggregator Services will get your book out on many platforms. While having a direct publishing set-up on each platform will give you more control, you also need to balance how much time you want to spend managing each account. The individual platforms require logins, file uploads, tax information, etc. When you work with an aggregator, you upload once and your book is distributed to their network.

There are many aggregators out there, and new ones seem to pop up pretty often. I am going to give you information on the ones that I have used and what my experience has been with each.

Smashwords

When I was starting out in 2015, and I knew I wanted to have my books available in libraries, I searched for "how to get my book into libraries." One of the initial results was an article about Overdrive and Baker&Taylor. These are two of the biggest services that libraries in the United States use to purchase books. When you drill down, libraries are a function of local municipal governments. They have limited budgets and a rigid procurement process. I knew I needed to be in Overdrive and Baker&Taylor to have a chance of getting into libraries. My next search led me to Smashwords.

Through Smashwords, I have been able to publish my eBooks to Overdrive, Baker&Taylor, Apple iBooks, Barnes & Noble Nook, and Kobo. This has been my go-to aggregator to get my eBooks into most of the retailers that aren't Amazon.

Cost

There are no upfront costs. Royalty rates will vary based on your retail price. When my eBooks were listed at $0.99, I made a 53% royalty. Now that they are listed for $3.99, I make 76%. When you enter your desired list price during setup, you will see multiple pie charts showing your royalty. Whether you sell your book directly through Smashwords, through an affiliate link, or a retailer, you will earn a different royalty split.

Set-Up Process

The interface for adding your title to Smashwords is a little outdated, but the questions are the same. You will need to provide your own ISBN. (Remember, if you used the ISBN that Amazon or another publishing service provides to you for "free" then you cannot take it and use it on another platform.)

As you go through the set-up, you will have the option to select all of the eBook file types you would like to have your book converted to. I always select all. Smashwords is my go-to for downloading ePub and Mobi copies of my eBooks when I need them. (See Google requirements in the last section.)

If there is an error with your document, Smashwords will notify you and keep your eBook out of their "premium catalog." The premium catalog is what gets you access to all of those retailers. Errors that you will see can include but are not limited to: formatting issues with your fonts or hyperlinks, indenting and spacing problems with the file, coding of tables and charts, etc.

When I am ready to put a new book up for pre-order, I will set it up with Smashwords first because of their thorough check and AutoVetter process. Usually, I miss one or two things like indenting or font formatting. I appreciate that they run this process. Once I get the all-clear on the document from Smashwords, I know I can add it to my other retailers.

Distribution & Reach

You can distribute to many retailers through Smashwords. This includes Amazon, but if your book is listed there through KDP it won't show twice. Your KDP listing will take precedence over the Smashwords listing. I like having my books directly on Amazon as well as Smashwords because I know that a good portion of my total sales still come from Amazon. I don't want to share my royalty cut from Amazon with Smashwords.

At the time of this printing, Smashwords has access to publish with 18 retailers as well as their own eCommerce store for books.

Having your book listed through Smashwords will get you that much closer to being in libraries, but you still need library patrons to request the book at their library.

Pros
- Easy to download Mobi, ePub, and other formats.
- AutoVetter checks everything!
- Your books are available on many retailers.

Cons
- Interface looks dated.
- Reporting lag between the day your book was purchased on a retailer, when it shows on your daily sales, and when it is paid.
- This aggregator will just work to get your eBooks into online retailers, not your print books.

StreetLib

Like Smashwords, StreetLib will distribute your book to many different retailers. The unique benefit to StreetLib is that you can get your book into international markets not offered through other direct platforms and aggregators.

At present, all of my books are only available in English. I may not be the first choice for readers on this platform who are looking for books in Spanish, Italian, or other global languages. However, I don't want to miss readers in these markets. They can still read my work in English.

Cost
Like the other self-publishing platforms that I have

mentioned, there is no direct cost to publish through StreetLib. You will need to bring your own ISBN. Each of the retailers that StreetLib works with will take a royalty; the rest will go to you.

Set-Up Process

Because this is a newer platform that not many self-published authors in the United States are making use of, I had a tough time with my first set-up on the system. There wasn't a lot of information available on the process. It was a little clunky, but I realized most of the issues I had were user-errors. After using the system a few times, I have been able to navigate it much easier.

StreetLib provides you with the option to take your finished manuscript and create an ePub file. Or you can directly upload your finished ePub file. Since I have already uploaded my book to Smashwords at this point in my process, I have my ePub file ready to upload directly. I would recommend doing this as my main difficulties were navigating the system to convert the document to ePub.

Distribution & Reach

Through StreetLib you can distribute to BajaLibros, Perlego, Unilibro, and many other eBook retailers. You can also distribute to Amazon, Barnes&Noble, Kobo, and other retailers that you will have access to through other channels. Deselect the retailers that you already distribute to as you go through the set-up process. This will prevent duplicate records and any confusion with reporting and royalties.

The primary reason I signed up with this service was to expand my international reach. To date, I have found the majority of my international sales come from Google Play. I will continue to work with StreetLib because it doesn't take much effort to add a book to the platform at this point in my process. For me, there are no disadvantages to having my books on this platform. I plan to use the sales data from StreetLib to inform any decisions regarding translations in the future.

Pros
- International exposure
- No up-front costs

Cons
- Clunky set-up, but you will get used to it after the first few books are uploaded.
- New markets that you will need to advertise in.

IngramSpark

IngramSpark is the self-publishing arm of the publishing powerhouse Ingram. It has one of the largest distribution networks for books and publishing. While you may not have the catalog or demand to support working with their flagship distribution company, their self-service platform is a great asset to self-published authors.

Cost

Unlike the other self-publishing platforms, there are direct and indirect costs associated with publishing through IngramSpark. As of January 2020, the cost to publish your eBook through their network is $25 and to set up one print book (either paperback or hardcover) is $49. However, they do have a bundle where you can set up both a print version and your eBook for $49. It is clear they know the power of perceived value and are getting more people to sign on for the bundle.

Like other self-publishing platforms, you should bring your own ISBN. They do offer a "free" one, however that means they are the publisher of record. Because IngramSpark has distribution with brick and mortar retail stores, you will also need to provide a barcode. You can use a barcode where the price is not set, but it will be less likely that a retail bookstore will carry your book.

Set-Up Process

The set-up process is much like the other systems with a few key differences. If you are setting up the bundle of a print edition and an eBook, the system streamlines the questions so you don't have to enter everything twice.

You will only be prompted to pay for your title once it

is approved. After you upload both your content and your cover art, it will go through a manual review process by Ingram.

To upload your print book content, you need to have a PDF file that has not been saved from Microsoft Word. This was a very specific requirement that I had to navigate when I first used IngramSpark. Usually, you can have a document in Microsoft Word and "Save As" a PDF. (You can do this with the Amazon KDP Paperback print templates that they provide for authors.) IngramSpark does not allow you to do this. You can hire a designer to format the book or learn how to use Adobe InDesign. I opted to use Scribus which is an Open Source (FREE!) document formatting software. It was a little clunky to learn, but since my content was text-only this was the best solution for me. I learned a new skill and saved some money in the process. If you have images, graphics, and charts in your book interior, you will want to work with a designer who has book formatting experience. (We'll discuss this more in Chapter 5.)

When you upload your eBook file to IngramSpark, you will have to upload it as an already converted ePub file, not a Microsoft Word document.

For most of my books I have uploaded to IngramSpark, for myself or my clients, I have seen edits kicked back. You will usually receive a response within

24 hours. An actual person sends you the notifications so you can ask for clarification if you are not sure what needs to be changed. Some of the issues have included: not saving the PDF as a single-page file, not saving the interior PDF in the correct color format, not enough bleed on the book cover, etc.

Once your interior and exterior files are approved by the IngramSpark team, you will be able to see a proof to review and give final approval. Look through every single page carefully. Once you approve the document, you will pay for your listing and any edits will also be subject to a fee.

This is the main drawback of this service. But, when you think about it, the team at IngramSpark will have to stop their presses and reset every time you change your files. The fee establishes an incentive for you to check, double-check, and triple-check that your files are accurate.

Within the set-up for your print book, you will have the option to select a paperback or hardcover version. The hardcover option is very appealing because it gives you another listing for your book and many readers prefer this format. At the time of this publication, in February 2020, this is currently not available through KDP or other self-publishing print-on-demand services.

Distribution & Reach

The biggest benefit to IngramSpark is the distribution. Your books can be found in Amazon, Barnes & Noble, Kobo, Walmart, Target, Overdrive, and other databases. The aggregators I have mentioned to date will help to distribute your eBooks, but IngramSpark can also distribute your print books to these retailers. For those of you who want to see your book on the shelves at your local store, IngramSpark is the aggregator you want to work with.

For eBooks, your metadata will be available within a few days. I have noticed books will show up for sale, and then the other metadata, like the cover image and description, will take a few days to appear on the retailer page.

I have set up clients with IngramSpark to have this as their one-stop publishing platform. Instead of having logins with Smashwords, Amazon, and IngramSpark, they only need the set-up with IngramSpark. This is for simplicity. If you want, you can publish your book on both Amazon KDP and IngramSpark. IngramSpark will still get you access to distribute with Amazon.

Your book may be listed on other retailers like Walmart and Target as well, but if you aren't selling any copies, they may remove the listing. Just as you will have the opportunity to sell your books into brick and mortar retail stores, the stores are not guaranteed to stock your book. You will need to reach out to your local independent and chain book stores to see if they will stock you as a local author.

The reasons that these brick and mortar stores will consider you are:

● The book is not printed by Amazon. Many brick and mortar stores will not consider stocking any books published by Amazon. (You get access to sell your book on Amazon, but you aren't printing with them).

● Your barcode with the price listed.

● Your books are returnable. This is a setting you will select during your set-up. You should select "returnable" on your book. If a store orders two cartons, but only sells one, they want to know they can send back the inventory.

● Your wholesale discount.

Up until now, you haven't had much of a say in the discount you are offering to retailers. When your eBook is over $2.99 on Amazon KDP, you can select a 35% or 70% royalty rate, but that isn't the same.

With IngramSpark, you can set your wholesale discount at 30% on up in the US and Canada and 35% on up for their other markets. This means that if your print book is $10.00, Barnes & Noble or another US retailer can buy it for $7.00, and sell it to the customer for your list price. They are taking inventory and making money off of your book. The retailers want to maximize what they make on each sale; this is good business. In an ideal world, everyone gets an even share. As Amazon commands more and more of the market share for all purchases, they can command a larger wholesale discount. (As an exception to this, if you have your eBook listed on Amazon as well as IngramSpark, your KDP listing will take precedence. You still make the 70% royalty rate if your book is over $2.99.)

Brick and mortar stores are facing thinner margins. They want a higher discount as well. Many brick and mortar stores will require a 50% wholesale discount before they will stock a book. In addition to warehousing, stores have overhead costs to cover like rent on their storefront and salaries for their employees. It is important to understand the pressures and business needs of everyone involved in selling your book.

For my books, I have set my discount to 30%. This is what works for me. You may decide to set your discount to 50% or somewhere in between. Be sure to do the math on your print cost, wholesale discount, and list price so you know what your expected royalty will be on each transaction.

With the additional costs and strategy involved in working with IngramSpark, you may decide it is not for you. After weighing the pros and cons, I decided to use IngramSpark to augment my offerings with paperback and hardcover formats for my books that were both available for pre-order. (I will go into further detail on the pre-order strategy in Chapter 6.)

Pros
- Access to distribute to many retailers.
- Hardcover options.
- Returnable books, which brick and mortar retailers require before they will stock your book. (While you may think this is a negative, this is a critical element to being able to pitch stores on carrying your title.)
- Offer your paperback or hardcover for pre-order.

Cons
- For print books, you cannot upload a PDF that was saved directly from a Microsoft Word Document.
- Can't see live data, at least 24-hour delay.
- Because your print books are print-on-demand, Amazon will sometimes show that the books are "out of stock" or take "1-2 months to ship". Just do a post to your followers that the estimated shipment times are worst case scenarios.
- Pay a fee to upload and edit.

Audiobook Self-Publishing Options

Audiobooks are becoming more and more popular. As a self-published author, this is a format that you should not ignore. While I will not go into all of the ins-and-outs of audiobook scripting, auditioning, production, and promotion in this book, I will give you information on the two top audiobook self-publishing aggregators: ACX and Findaway Voices.

ACX

ACX stands for Audiobook Creation Exchange. It is another subsidiary of Amazon. Just as KDP is the self-service platform for eBooks and paperbacks, ACX is their self-service platform to publish audiobooks.

Cost

Compared to other book formats, there are more costs associated with audiobooks. Quality audio equipment and mixing software is not cheap, but there are low-cost or free alternatives you can consider if you have the patience.

There are no direct costs associated with uploading your audiobook to ACX. They will take a cut of the royalties. The rate will differ based on whether you upload your audiobook exclusively with ACX (you get 40% of the sale) or if you plan to list your audiobook elsewhere (you get 25% of the sale). Sound familiar? Amazon understands how to align the incentives to tempt authors into exclusivity.

The other costs associated with your audiobook will be in the narration and production. ACX will provide you with the ability to find a narrator through their system.

You can either pay a flat fee for their work or through a royalty split with the voice actor. Whoever you work with should provide you with finished and formatted audio files. If you narrate and edit the files yourself, you don't have to share any of the royalties, but you may have some up-front costs for the equipment and software.

You will not have any say over the price of the audiobook. You may think this would lead ACX to price it too low to see any return; this has not been my experience. The books are supposed to be priced based on the size of the files. The longer books have more files and take up more storage on the Amazon servers. What I have found is that all of the books I have with ACX are listed at $19.95, regardless of the file size. My theory is that ACX prices the one-time purchase higher so that the Audible subscription looks that much more tempting to the consumer. But that is just my take. You will get paid whether a user is purchasing the audiobook outright or using their monthly Audible credits.

Set-Up Process
If your book is already published on Amazon, you can "claim your title" so your audiobook will show as an additional purchase option next to your eBook or print formats. If you are publishing through KDP, you will already have a single sign-on for Amazon to log into ACX. If you published through an aggregator, you will

still be able to search, find, and claim your title. The purple button to "assert your title" or "claim your title" is visible on the homepage of your ACX dashboard. For the audiobooks I have developed, I have never had a problem claiming a title.

Instead of uploading a single file, like you did with the eBook and paperback, you will upload each chapter or section as a separate audio file. You will need to have opening and closing credits as well as an audio sample.

Once you have all of your audio files uploaded and your audio cover in the system, you will submit for review. A real person will review the files, not a computer. This ensures quality, but it usually takes a week or so. In some cases, I have had to wait the maximum time of 10-14 business days. Patience is key here.

Distribution & Reach

ACX allows you to publish your audiobook directly to Amazon, Audible, and Apple. These are arguably the most recognizable brands that authors would love to have their audiobooks available through. Because you will be able to link up your title, when a customer goes to your book's page on Amazon, they will be able to see all of the formats, including audiobooks, to select from. This makes it easier for the consumer and adds credibility to your title.

Pros

● Produce and publish your audiobook to Amazon, Audible, and Apple.

● Option to do a royalty split with a narrator. ACX will handle all the back-end payments.

● Free codes to drive new listeners and reviews.

Cons

● Very strict review process – this is a pro in some regards because we all want good quality. But at times it can feel like an excessive number of edits.

● No access to libraries.

● No control over pricing.

Findaway Voices

Findaway Voices is another aggregator for audiobook self-publishers. They work in much the same way as ACX, except that their network has a larger reach and includes libraries!

Cost

Same deal as the rest (except IngramSpark). You don't pay any direct fees to Findaway, but they will take a cut of the royalties. You should bring your own ISBN. (Yes. I'm beating this horse until it is dead because I believe in it that much!)

Set-Up Process

When you first create an account with Findaway Voices,

they immediately put you through a series of questions about your book. This questionnaire starts with a voice actor form wizard to connect you with a narrator. If you need a narrator, this is great. If you already have your audio files because you worked directly with a voice actor or you narrated the book yourself, you will need to state this clearly when prompted for details about your ideal voice actor. An actual human will review each of these form submissions. You will then receive an email in a day or so saying that you can now upload your audio.

Just like with ACX, you can be paired with a voice actor or bring your own files. When you are ready to submit, you will need to check to see if your book is approved. When I have used their service, I have not received any confirmation or edits.

Distribution & Reach
Findaway has distribution through Audiobooks.com, Overdrive, Baker&Taylor, Apple, Amazon, and many other retailers. They continue to add more options each day as well. If you are also publishing through ACX you will need to deselect Amazon and Audible from your distribution when you go through the Findaway Voices set-up. Remember, if you plan to publish with ACX and Findaway, you will need to indicate on your ACX set-up that this is a non-exclusive deal.

The great thing about the set-up with Findaway is that

you can set a separate price for libraries. They suggest making it 3x your retail price since libraries will get a license to lend out the audiobook multiple times. I have set my audiobooks at a lower cost because I feel that is my way of supporting libraries. When you see sales come in from libraries you will see either the year-long license or a one-time use fee. Depending on the library system they may elect to pick these different pricing structures.

Pros
- Distribution to all major audiobook retailers.
- Access to have your audiobook in libraries.
- Control over retail pricing AND library pricing.

Cons
- Newer, likely working out some kinks in their communication platform.
- When you go with Findaway, that means you are non-exclusive with ACX and will get a lower rate from that platform.

Now that we have covered the major platforms for publishing your book, you can start to make decisions on which you will use. Will you be an Amazon-Only author or will you Publish Wide? If you are going Wide, which platforms will best meet your needs and the vision you have for your book? Write down your vision for the book and which platforms interest you the most. Read their terms and conditions and check out reviews from other independent authors before you sign up.

After making all of the decisions that we reviewed in the first four chapters, it is time to format your book. Each platform will provide you with a style guide and details on how to format your manuscript before uploading it. Let's learn how to take this step with your book.

Chapter 5:

How do I Format my Book?

I stated in the previous chapter that you should have your book formatted before you upload it. But you need to know what platform you are working with to make sure you have formatted it correctly.

As I mentioned about IngramSpark, you cannot upload a PDF that was created and saved from Microsoft Word for your print books. KDP will allow this. This is just one example of why you want to know which platforms you will use before you format your book.

The great thing about having your book on any word processor is that it is easy to copy and paste the text into another document if you need to. The trick here is that if you copy and paste the text, you may copy over any formatting errors. But if you copy and paste as plain text, you will lose all of your *italicized* or **bolded** text. That means you need to pay close attention to details. This process should be meticulous. You didn't just spend a year (or more) on your book to rush through this critical step.

Below are different tools that you can use as you format your manuscript. There are more options available for a fee that I have not used, which is why they are not listed here. Do your research before investing in any tool and, if available, make use of their free-trial options to see if the added cost will be worth the investment.

Google Docs

When you are writing your book, Google Docs can be a good option. As with Microsoft Word, you can format text by headings. This will be helpful when you add a table of contents. (You will be required to have a linked table of contents in all of your eBooks.)

If you download the Google Docs app on your smartphone, you'll have access to your manuscript anywhere you have WiFi access. Because the document will autosave you will have some protection from one of the worst things to happen to any author: unsaved changes getting lost.

The text won't be able to go directly from Google Docs to upload into KDP or Smashwords. First, you'll need to download the manuscript into Microsoft Word. However, you will only be able to download the document from Google Docs into the ".docx" format for Microsoft Word. This means that once you open the document, you will need to save it again as a ".doc" file, preferably the Microsoft Word 1997-2003 version. The ".doc" file is the easiest to format without any blocks and produces the fewest errors when you upload it into Smashwords. For this reason, I have always started each manuscript in Microsoft Word.

Microsoft Word

Since Microsoft Word is the most widely used word processor, you might start here instead. By skipping the download process with Google Docs, you will save yourself a step.

Formatting your eBook in Word

You can format your manuscript for eBook conversion in Microsoft Word with only a few limitations. The same file can be uploaded to Amazon KDP and most of the self-publishing aggregators. Only Google Books and IngramSpark require that you provide an already converted ePub file. I use Smashwords to generate my ePub files as I mentioned in Chapter 4. Because of this, I start in Microsoft Word and then save my converted files from Smashwords. (I have created a flowchart to help you make sure you aren't missing any steps here at AuthorYourAmbition.com/Self-Publishing-Flowchart)

In addition to providing a linked table of contents at the beginning of your book, you will need to keep a few other things in mind when formatting your eBook in Word:

• As I mentioned above, the final file type should be ".doc" NOT ".docx".

• When you are indenting your paragraphs, they all need to be indented in the same manner. By this, I mean that after a few paragraphs of your hitting "tab" to indent the paragraph, Microsoft Word will catch on and start to auto-indent for you. In the Word document, you won't be able to tell the difference. In your ePub file the paragraph indentations will look different. When you are done with the book, you will either need to go back and force indent every paragraph or make sure every paragraph is auto-indented. For the entire book.

• Check your fonts. The second book that I released was a collection of short stories. I had each story set in a different font; I thought I was being very clever with the typography. This produced errors in the Smashwords AutoVetter and resulted in my eBook being flagged as containing errors on Amazon with a big orange error message on the book's purchase page. Have your book all in one font. Use italics and bold where you need to.

● Images and Tables. Be careful and very selective with any images or charts you want to include in the eBook. How critical is this picture to the book? You may format it to be centered, but after file conversion, it may force align to be left-justified. Is that a deal-breaker? Also, you cannot have any tables in your ePub document. You will need to save the table as an image and embed it as a picture.

Formatting your Print Book in Word

This section only applies to those who will print their paperback through KDP. I've tried to set up the formatting in the Word document manually. It was a nightmare. Then I looked on the KDP website and found their templates. This was a lifesaver. Based on the dimensions I wanted for the book, I was able to pick the corresponding template that already had the correct bleed, trim, and pagination programmed in.

When you select a template, pick one with sample content. There will be 10 "chapters" included along with a Table of Contents, Title Page, Acknowledgements, and a Copyright Page. (The Copyright Page will be empty, so you will still need to add in the details.) Before moving any of your manuscript into the document, scroll to the end of the template. Copy the final chapter multiple times so you have extra "sample content goes here" chapters. You will likely have more than 10 chapters in your book and the beginning of each chapter will be set to have the same formatting and spacing.

Next, you should take your content and copy it, without formatting, into the document. Be careful to not erase any of the spacing. Because you will be copying and pasting without formatting, I recommend that you only copy over a few paragraphs at a time so you can easily add back in any italics or bold typesetting. When I do this, I usually put the text into Grammarly one last time as a final check.

Because you will be copying and pasting, be very careful to not skip any paragraphs or enter any content twice. This is not something to do while "multitasking." I recommend that you take breaks so that you can keep your concentration. You know your capacity for distraction better than anyone else, so plan accordingly.

When you are done, save the Word document and then hit "Save As" and create a PDF file to upload to Amazon. You can "Save As" a PDF from ".doc" or ".docx" if you have set up the template yourself. The templates that Amazon provides are ".docx".

Look through the PDF before you upload it. You will also have an opportunity to review the proof before approving.

This method works best for text-only books.

Scribus

For publishing your print book with IngramSpark, you will need to create your PDF in a software that is not Microsoft Word. As I looked into options for formatting software, I decided to give Scribus a try over more expensive options. Scribus is open source software and free to use. The user interface looks a little dated, but it gets the job done. I found videos on YouTube to learn how to set up the template and saved a considerable amount of money along the way. I still would have had to learn another formatting software, so this was a win for me. (For comparison, Adobe InDesign would have been $20.99/month.)

Once you have the template set up for the trim, bleed, right pages, and left pages, you can start to enter your content just like you would do in Microsoft Word. Remember to only copy and paste a few paragraphs at a time. This software can be a little clunky, so be very careful as you format.

Once you are done, give it a thorough review before you export. Keep the working file and the PDF with your saved files in case you need to go back and make any edits. After you have checked everything, you will need to export to PDF and set the color to print quality. When you "Export to PDF," the window will show your page parameters. You will need to select the tab at the top that reads "Color" to change the color settings for the PDF.

Hiring A Professional

So far, I've told you about how you can format your own book, but my examples have been limited to books that are text-only. Most novels and works of fiction fall into this category. But what if you are writing a book that needs illustrations or a non-fiction book that requires charts and graphs? Audiences expect to see a cohesive visual theme on the interior and exterior of books. If you have multiple charts, they should all have the same stylization. If you are writing a how-to book that will have spaces for journaling or exercises for your reader to work through, how will you design that?

If you have design experience, you may be able to this yourself in Adobe InDesign or another program that has similar design capabilities. If you don't have these skills, then you will need to hire someone. If you have a text-only book, but you don't have the time to learn a new skill or the patience to master new software, then you can hire someone as well.

In general, you can expect your expenses in hiring someone to format your book to increase with the amount of design needed. If you are hiring someone to format your text-only book this could be $50-200 depending on the length of the book and the experience of the designer.

For a book where you need tables and charts or illustrations, you can expect to pay more. Here are some things to consider when you are looking to hire a designer to format the interior of your book:

- **Recommendations**. Ask your network if they know a designer who can format a book. Someone with graphic design and InDesign experience could do this for you. But you want to work with someone who has some book experience because they will know about pagination, left-right shift, and other factors specific to book interiors. Once you have some recommendations, look for someone who has formatted in your genre or at least your style of book. If you have a non-fiction book that will have multiple charts and images and you hire someone who has only formatted text-only books, you may not get the result that you want.

- **Availability and Schedule**. First and foremost, you need to see if they are available. If you have a deadline in mind, but they aren't available to work with you for a few months, then you will either need to move back your timeline or find someone else who can meet your goal. After you tell the designer about your project, you should ask how long they think it will take. Someone who gives a thoughtful response and builds in additional buffer time has experience in book formatting. Someone who says they will meet your deadline blindly without elaborating on their process should be a red flag. Maybe they are just trying to sign you on, or they think they will be able to do an "all-nighter" or two to get the work done. This will result in errors and make the process longer than it needs to be.

• **Price**. Ask for their pricing based on the length of the book (both pages and word count) as well as what your vision is for the number of images or charts. You should provide the length in terms of "my book is X pages in Microsoft Word and Y words." If you used Google Docs or another word processor, switch them out. This gives them an idea of how many print pages they will be working with. After you discuss the concept for your book, they may give you a rate based on the number of "design pages." This means pages that will need a high level of design elements. If you have ten mostly-text pages to every one design page you can start to calculate the cost.

• **Experience and Examples**. Ask to see examples of their previous work. This lets you get a feel for what they are capable of doing. Keep in mind that the designer may have been asked to do the interior in a very specific way for a client, so it may not reflect their design aesthetic as much as it reflects their previous client's desires.

• **Expectations**. Will they just be formatting your print book or can they prepare the eBook files as well? Will they be doing the cover design for you? How will they send concepts for you to review and approve or provide feedback on? Communicate early and often to avoid confusion that can be costly to your timeline and budget.

I have worked with several designers who have done amazing interior formatting work. A great designer can transform your words into the book that you have envisioned.

At this point, you have a finished book with print/download ready files. So, what is your next step? Well, it is time to put your book on sale!

Chapter 6:

How Should I Price my Book and What is a Pre-Order?

Your book is written, edited, and formatted. You have a finished product that you are ready to introduce to the world. Now you need to figure out how you are going to give your book the best debut.

Some of you who write for the love of your craft may find this part difficult. I struggled for years with the idea that any strategies to optimize sales and royalties would sully my art. This is a symptom of the fear of success, imposter syndrome, and other psychological aspects of being an entrepreneur.

If you are nervous about pricing your book, just know

that I have met amazing authors who dedicate their lives to their craft, and they still manage to make a living from their work. You can write to create art, but if you ignore pricing and your launch strategy, no one will ever get to experience it.

Pricing

The great thing about self-publishing is that you have control over your list price (except for audiobooks with ACX). You decide what you think a fair price is for your book, and the self-publishing platforms will show you exactly what kind of royalty you can expect to make on each sale. It is unique for you as an author to have this level of control. Traditionally published authors do not have this option, this is where self-publishing can be a great asset to you.

Set Your Price

When I was ready to publish my first book, I researched how to structure my price. I looked at other science fiction thrillers on Amazon to see what they were charging. At the time, I had trouble thinking that anyone would spend more than a dollar on anything I created. I was a "no one" in the book world and I needed to build my audience. I was also so frugal that I couldn't put myself in the mindset of a reader who would part with their money to read my book. These thoughts and worries are normal for new authors. But this kind of thinking does you no favors.

There are an endless number of blogs and podcasts that will give you advice on how to price your book. One piece of advice that I followed was to keep my price at $0.99 for my first two books. I needed to build a readership, and I thought a low price would entice more readers. What I didn't realize was the lower price signaled to readers that my book wasn't worth very much. Your price is more than just "a good deal," it is an indicator of the value and quality that the reader can expect.

Be sure to research what established writers in your genre are charging for their books. You should also review the prices for your fellow new authors. This can let you know what readers expect to see and also what they are used to paying for a book.

When my first two books came out, I set them to $0.99. At the 35% royalty rate with KDP, I earned $0.34 per book. No one can make a living off of that. Looking back now, I should have kept the books at this price for a limited time and pushed readers to purchase while prices were low. Now that I have multiple titles out, I know I can charge $3.99 for my eBooks and $11.99 for my paperback books without worrying about how "established" my books appear on the different retailers. Years of experience and sales have helped to bolster my confidence. As you research your genre, you may find that another price point suits your book.

Kindle Unlimited Options

The limited-time offer that I referenced above wouldn't have been easy for me to execute on my first two books. Because I wasn't enrolled in Kindle Select, I would have had to go into the set-up for the books on KDP and set a new price. Then, on the date that the promotion was over, I would have had to log back in and change the price again. For authors who enroll in Kindle Select, they can set-up a limited time discount with ease. A countdown timer will show on the book's Amazon page to press the urgency of the deal.

With Kindle Select, I also could have listed my book for free as a limited-time offer. There are specific lists and rankings for free books on Amazon that appeal to readers looking for deals and freebies. This can be an effective way to get your book out to lots of people very quickly. This also makes it easier to ask early readers and reviewers to "buy" your book when it is listed for free so they can leave a "verified" review.

If you have weighed the pros and cons of being part of Kindle Select and Kindle Unlimited and have decided that this option works for you, then you can easily access these limited-time deals. Readers need a deadline to take action. That's why these programs work to your advantage. If you decide that you want to Publish Wide, you can still run price promotions; it will just take more effort on your part to manually make the price changes and promote the discount yourself.

A third option would be to launch in Kindle Unlimited for the first 90 days to access these programs. You will need to opt-out before the 90 days renew or you will be locked into the program for another three months. Because your book will have to be exclusive with Amazon during this time, you will miss out on the first 90 days of promotion on other platforms.

Setting Discounts

Beyond the scope of what is or is not available through Kindle Select, as a business owner you need to write down your policy on discounts. Your books are a business and you need to be able to find the strategy that works for you and stick to it. I've seen authors run from one "shiny object" to the next in the hopes that it will be the magic cure to their declining book sales. Discounts should be a strategic part of your pricing and marketing strategy, not something that you decide on a whim.

As with any business, you have set your price for your product based on what you think the market will bear, what your expenses are to produce the book, and what you will need to earn in royalties to cover your other expenses. Don't sell yourself, or your book, short.

Discounting Strategies to Consider:

- **Discount for Early Adopters**: This can be something as simple as "Pre-Sale Pricing" where you charge a lower amount for your book when it is on

Pre-Sale. You'll need to promote that the price will increase when the book is released. This can drive up your Pre-Sale orders. It also gives your audience a clear reason to purchase now instead of waiting. Pre-Sale Pricing rewards your early adopters by giving them a better deal. You never want to penalize your early adopters. If you charge one price during Pre-Sale and then discount the book after it is released, some of your most loyal and eager fans will see that they paid more. This makes them think that perhaps that they should have waited to purchase. Penalizing your biggest fans and early adopters means they may wait to buy your next book until it is on discount or move on to another author altogether.

● **Seasonal Discounts**: Every year around late November – PEOPLE LOSE THEIR MINDS. A purchase that was too expensive the week prior is now a steal because there is a $10 off discount. The human brain is a great machine, but all rational thought seems to evaporate at the mention of sales. Black Friday through Cyber Monday (Cyber Week now) is a sales and discounting blitz. You will be competing with every other retailer who is discounting at this time. But, if you are only offering your books at full price, will you miss out on the potential to sell more books? Think strategically about how you want to participate (or not) in the holiday discounts and how it will impact your profit margin. You may find a better approach by connecting with a local independent bookstore to participate in Small Business Saturday and offer your books at a discounted rate to encourage foot traffic into these stores.

• **Series Releases**: If you are planning to write a series of books, you may consider discounting the earlier books in the series as the next book is released. Many readers prefer to read a series of books in order. If you are promoting book three, your group of readers is limited to the people who have read books one and two in the series. To drive sales for book three, you need to get more readers to pick up book one. Offering a discount on the first books can build excitement around the series and bring more readers into the story.

• **"Perma" Discount**: The price that you set anchors the book to a certain value. One tactic that I have seen in other industries that can be applied to books is a "Perma" discount, short for permanent discount. Let's say you've done your pricing research and you want to sell your eBook for $2.99. You can set the list price at $3.99 or $4.99 and then discount to $2.99. By doing this, you anchor the value of the book to that higher price while you earn the amount that you planned to make all along. This also gives the reader a feeling that they have just scored a great deal. The downside of the Perma discounts is that there is no deadline to purchase by. You can continually rotate through discounts and have limited periods where the book is at full price, but that is a lot more for you to manage.

Write out your pricing and discount strategy. Keep that

piece of paper in a place where you can find it. You will get opportunities to participate in sales throughout the year from your self-publishing platforms. You will see other authors discounting or trying something clever with their pricing and will be tempted to copy them right away. If you see a new strategy, research it, think about it, and only if you have given it at least a month to consider, add it to your written pricing and discount strategy document. I've created a version of this for you to use. Access it at AuthorYourAmbition.com/Pricing-and-Discount-Strategy.

Remember, your price will be an external indication of value. You worked hard to write your book, edit it, and publish it. You set the price.

Pre-Sale

I've mentioned the concept of a Pre-Sale or Pre-Orders throughout this book. Again, there are many circular mental paths that you will need to walk as you learn and plan to self-publish your book. A Pre-Sale or Pre-Order is when a reader can order your book before it is released.

Do you remember when the *Harry Potter* books were still coming out? I sure do! I was a huge fanatic. I went to the midnight release parties at Barnes & Noble for books 4-7. I loved the excitement of knowing that the next volume would soon be released. But I also worried that I would stand in line with an eye-liner lightning bolt on my forehead only to learn that the book was sold out. Through the magic of a new website, Amazon.com, and parents who supported my reading addiction, they were able to pre-order the book. I had a freshly printed copy to read the day it came out. Think about that on a global scale. *Harry Potter* is still one of the most successful book series of all time. The excitement and demand for each new book helped to make that happen.

While your book may not be the next *Harry Potter*, you can leverage the Pre-Sale strategy to your advantage. The strategy here is that you want to have a surge of book sales the day that your book is released. The Pre-Sale strategy allows you to do this because every book you sell during the Pre-Sale period will count in the Amazon (and other retailer) ranking system as a book purchase at 12:01 am the morning that your book is released. If you get a dozen Pre-Sales, you realize 12 book sales the morning of your release. If you get a hundred Pre-Sales, you rank for 100 book sales the morning of your release. And so on. This wave of book sales will help to propel you to the top of the rankings for your genre. When you are ranked higher, more readers will discover your book. This leads to more sales. It is a very positive feedback loop to get into.

Build Momentum

As you announce details about your book, you want to build momentum. Release the title, then the cover art. Staggering these announcements gives you more to say to your audience. I would recommend that as soon as you have the final cover art and your interior files, you launch for Pre-Sale. With each announcement, you can build followers and e-mail subscribers. If you want to optimize further, you can add the book as a TBD title, TBD cover, and TBD description on Goodreads so that your followers will get updates as soon as the details are filled in and the book is released.

As the release date draws closer, you will want to build excitement and buzz around the book to drive more Pre-Sales. Some ways to do this include:

- Select quotes from the book
- Reviews from your Beta Readers or ARC Readers
- Character introductions
- Daily countdown posts
- Early rankings posts
- Thank you to those who have Pre-Ordered
- Opening your first box of printed copies
- The list can go on and on

Incentivize Pre-Orders

One way to drive Pre-Orders is to give people a reason to take action now. People tell themselves that they will remember to buy your book later. They won't. They are busy and have other priorities. You want to give them a reason to order immediately. As mentioned in the previous section, you can offer them a better price. If this is not in line with your pricing and discount strategy or will be too manual to execute, you have other options.

One strategy to consider is giving anyone who Pre-Orders a bonus. Whatever this bonus is, be sure it is easy to execute. You will be busy marketing and promoting your book. You should also ensure it is affordable for you to execute. Don't promise everyone who Pre-Orders an extravagant gift, then you have to pay for the gift plus shipping.

I recommend that you offer a digital bonus. This can be a series of worksheets that align with your non-fiction book topic. Or a side-story that is in the same world as your book series. This can also be an exclusive author Q&A. There are many possibilities. Get creative, you are an author!

One key thing to remember is that this bonus is for everyone who Pre-Orders. Don't think you're being fancy and enter names into a raffle. There are very strict laws around lotteries or contests of chance. If you require someone to spend money (Pre-Order) as a condition of winning, then this could get you into trouble. If you give everyone who Pre-Orders this bonus, then you are in the clear.

But how do you know who Pre-Ordered and who didn't? For this, you need to provide clear instructions on how the reader can send in proof of purchase. Don't ask for a receipt. This can threaten some people. A receipt can have identifying information on it. A receipt is a proof of purchase, but so is a screenshot of the Amazon or Barnes & Noble thank you page. Either will work, but if you say "proof of purchase" people will know they have an option. To handle these messages, set up a second email address or inbox. If you already have an email address for your author business, that can work too. Give specific directions to send a proof of purchase to that email address. These instructions should be on your Pre-Order marketing assets (posts, ads, tweets, etc.).

When these are sent in, you should respond with your offer as soon as you can and thank them for their support. Keep track of these emails in a separate folder. Be sure to email them again once the book is released to remind them to read it. You can ask for a review in that message as well. Then the transaction is complete. This does not mean that you can email them about every little promotion that you do moving forward. For that, they would need to opt into promotional messages. When you email them based on a specific transaction you are in the clear.

Don't Make People Wait Too Long
Every author out there will tell you their opinion about

how long your Pre-Order period should last. If you are aiming to get your book into brick and mortar retailers, you need at least a six-month Pre-Order period. Stores have longer procurement cycles than online retailers. Six-months allows you time to build demand and promote your book to these stores.

Some authors will put their book on Pre-Order for months. Others just a few weeks. I have found that if my book is on Pre-Order for too long, potential buyers will put off their purchase. They think they can just order later. Or worse, they order, receive nothing, go back through their recent purchases, wonder why nothing arrived, and cancel the order to get their money back. (Don't assume the average reader will remember your book release date.)

You should do at least a 4-week Pre-Order based on my experience. This gives you time to build momentum, but it will still push readers to buy right away. People will forget if they don't see your posts; you will need to remind them often throughout the Pre-Order period.

I am friends with a fellow author who supports my work gladly. I announced the Pre-Order for my last book after she had recently moved to a new city. A few weeks later, she posted online that she was looking for a new book to read so she could relax after weeks of packing and unpacking. She specifically wanted a science fiction novel with a strong female heroine. A mutual friend of ours posted a response, "Get M.K.'s new book!" with the link. She wrote back right away and said she had missed my announcement. This doesn't make her a bad friend. She was living her life and missed one of my posts. You will need to remind people to take action. If you have enough time, you can ensure that your message gets out to all of your most dedicated readers.

You will need to find a balance to make sure that you don't overdo it though. You can't post "buy my book" once an hour, every hour, for your entire Pre-Order period. That is annoying and you will probably lose a lot of followers and friends. With each launch, you will get a feel for how much is too much or too little for your audience.

There are many strategies that you can employ to ensure a successful Pre-Sale and book launch. The important thing is to have a plan and take note of what is/isn't working. Just because one strategy worked for a different author, doesn't mean it will work for you, and vice versa. See what works, adapt, and take the learnings into your next book launch.

Chapter 7:

Continuous Learning and Ambitious Goals

At this point, you should be able to select the formats for your book, edit it, format it, publish it, and create your pricing plan. You have accomplished something that so many people only ever talk about. You wrote a book and published it! But the journey doesn't stop here. You'll need to learn and grow to continue your success.

Keep Learning

One of the biggest factors in my success as an author and independent publisher has been my ability to keep learning. You will find that there is so much more to self-publishing than can be encapsulated in one book (or volume of books). Once you feel like you have a handle on your business, a new platform will pop up or policies will change. There are many books, newsletters, podcasts, YouTube Channels, and online personalities out there all giving great information to self-published authors. Find a handful that are targeted to your genre and business.

For me, I listen to the following podcasts to stay up-to-date on self-publishing news and trends. I can listen while I work out or if I have a long drive.

- The Creative Penn with Joanna Penn
- Inside Independent Book Publishing with IBPA
- Go Publish Yourself from IngramSpark

You may prefer to read a newsletter or follow an expert on social media. There will be some trial and error to find the right mix for you. If you listen to podcasts, be sure to branch out and follow some new voices every so often.

Goals

In your mind, you may know that the chances of being a best-seller are small. With so many books on the market, how can your book break out from the masses and rise to the top? Your brain knows the challenges ahead of you. But your imagination, your heart, wants those things. You wrote a great book. You want to believe that if you could just get the right person to read it that it will be the top book of the year.

These dreams are what drive us all to write the best books that we can. But they are dreams. What you need to focus on are your goals and the systems you put in place to reach them. Set goals for yourself in increments that are realistic, but will still push you to work for more. The measuring stick for how many copies readers have to purchase for you to be a best-seller moves every day. The scale is relative to other books in your category. If you write a science-fiction horror book and release it one day with 100 pre-orders, you may be the best-seller that day. If you happen to release it the same day as Stephen King, well your 100 pre-orders aren't going to touch his numbers. Don't pick your goals based on arbitrary designations.

Make your goals measurable and time-based. From the example above, if you set a goal to sell 100 books during Pre-Sale, then you know exactly when you need to have this accomplished. Maybe you set another goal to reach 50 reviews on Goodreads within one month of the book-release date. Again, this is measurable and time-based.

Set ambitious goals. But don't keep your head in the clouds either. It's a fine balance to strike. I won't make you any promises that one thing or a specific combination of tasks will lead to a certain measure of success. The number of variables involved are too great. But I can tell you that if you focus on the details that I have outlined in this book, that you will be able to hold your book and call yourself an author.

Chapter 8:
Your Publishing Plan

Throughout this book, you have learned many things. Self-publishing can be overwhelming, and you will soon uncover even more that needs to happen after your book is published to continue to market and promote it. For now, focus on your publishing plan. Just as with your pricing plan, write down each of the items that you have selected for your strategy:

- What formats will you publish your book in?
- Who will be your editor(s)?
- Will you aim to publish in retail stores or primarily online?
- Do you want your book accessible to libraries?
- Which retailers do you want to get your book into?

- What platforms will you use to publish your book?
- Who will put the finishing touches on your manuscript files for publication?
- What will be your pricing and discounting strategy?
- How will you leverage Pre-Sales to launch your book?

Know your plan and stick to it, don't keep looking at the new shiny objects. Investigate first, then think on it before making a move. Claim your FREE Publishing Plan at AuthorYourAmbition.com/Publishing-Plan.

And don't forget to celebrate your book when it goes live! It is a huge moment!

Bibliography:

Watson, Amy. "U.S. Book Industry - Statistics & Facts." Statista. January 16, 2019.
https://www.statista.com/topics/1177/book-market/

Perrin, Andrew. "One-in-five Americans now listen to audiobooks." Pew Research Center. September 25, 2019.
https://www.pewresearch.org/fact-tank/2019/09/25/one-in-five-americans-now-listen-to-audiobooks/.

Resources:

AuthorYourAmbition.com
Self-Publisher's Legal Handbook by Helen Sedwick
Self-Publishing Formula with Mark Dawson
The Creative Penn with Joanna Penn
Kindlepreneur with Dave Chesson

M.K. Williams is an author and independent publisher. She left her career in sports marketing to pursue writing and publishing full-time in 2019. She has published three novels, one financial workbook, and a collection of short stories. In addition to publishing her own works, she has helped established companies bring their information to the masses through publishing books under their own brands. She focuses on helping aspiring authors realize their dreams. When she isn't writing she enjoys running and reading in her spare time.

Thank you so much for reading *Self-Publishing for the First Time Author*. I hope that you enjoyed reading it as much as I enjoyed writing it.

If you found this book helpful, please take a moment to leave a review. This helps other first-time authors find this book to help them on their journey.

Claim your FREE Self-Publishing Checklist at AuthorYourAmbition.com/Checklist.

I would love to hear from you as you continue to publish your books to hear what has worked for you and how you have put this information to use. You can reach me at authoryourambition@gmail.com.